# Cambridge checkpoint

Cambridge Assessment
International Education
Endorsed for learner support

## Lower Secondary
## English
## WORKBOOK

### 7

T0272717

John Reynolds

Boost

HODDER
EDUCATION

Third-party websites, publications and resources referred to in this publication have not been endorsed by Cambridge Assessment International Education.

The Publishers would like to thank the following for permission to reproduce copyright material:

**Text credits**

**p.3** Hostelbookers.com/blog. **p.11** extract from *Wonderful Adventures of Mrs Seacole in Many Lands* by Mary Seacole (1857). Penguin UK. **p.14** extract from *I Can't Stay Long* by Laurie Lee (2015). Reproduced with permission of Curtis Brown Ltd, London, on behalf of the Estate of Laurie Lee. Copyright © The Estate of Laurie Lee 1975. **p.17** extract from *Quite Early One Morning* by Dylan Thomas, published by New Directions Publishing Corporation, New York, 1954 Copyright © 1937, 1945, 1955, 1956, 1962, 1965, 1966, 1967, 1971, 1977 The Trustees for the Copyrights of Dylan Thomas. **p.21** extract from *The Hound of the Baskervilles* by Arthur Conan Doyle (1902). Penguin Random House. **p.24** extract from *Vanity fair: a novel without a hero* (Vol. 2) by W. M. Thackeray (1848). Harper & Brothers. **p.28** extract from *A Christmas Carol and other Christmas Books* by Charles Dickens (1905). **p.45** 'The Man, the Boy and the Donkey' C. W. Eliot (Ed.). (1910). *The Harvard Classics* (Vol. 50). P. F. Collier & Son. **pp.47–48** 'King of the Birds' by Brishti Bandyopadhyay. Retrieved from https://www.pitara.com/fiction-for-kids/folktales/king-of-the-birds/. Used with permission. **pp.54–55, 57** 'High and Lifted Up' by Mike Krath. East of the Web and contributors. Retrieved from http://www.eastoftheweb.com/short-stories/UBooks/HighLift.shtml. Used with permission. **p.61** extract from 'The Five Orange Pips' from *The Adventures of Sherlock Holmes* by Arthur Conan Doyle. **pp.63, 66** Ghost Stories: 'Cow's Head: An Ukrainian Ghost Story' retold by S. E. Schlosser. Copyright 2021. All rights reserved. Retrieved from https://americanfolklore.net/folklore/2010/07/cows_head.html. **p.72** 'Important Notice' by Brian Waddell from *The Works 2: Poems on Every Subject and for Every Occasion*, edited by Brian Moses and Pie Corbett (Macmillan Children's Books, 2002). **pp.73–74** 'The Last Wolf Speaks from the Zoo' by Pie Corbett from *The Works 2: Poems on Every Subject and for Every Occasion*, edited by Brian Moses and Pie Corbett (Macmillan Children's Books, 2002). **p.77** 'I'm Nobody' by Emily Dickinson. **p.79** 'Who Has Seen the Wind?' by Christina Rossetti. **p.79** 'Afternoon on a Hill' by Edna St Vincent Millay. **p.81** Barack Obama election victory speech in Chicago 2008 https://en.wikisource.org/wiki/Barack_Obama%27s_2008_election_victory_speech. **pp.83–84** extract from *Romeo and Juliet* by William Shakespeare. **pp.87–88** 'Hurricane Hits England' by Grace Nichols. **p.90** extract from *The Island of Dr Moreau* by H. G. Wells (1896).

**Photo credit**

**p.33** © Vera NewSib/stock.adobe.com

**Acknowledgements**

Every effort has been made to trace all copyright holders, but if any have been inadvertently overlooked, the Publishers will be pleased to make the necessary arrangements at the first opportunity.

Although every effort has been made to ensure that website addresses are correct at time of going to press, Hodder Education cannot be held responsible for the content of any website mentioned in this book. It is sometimes possible to find a relocated web page by typing in the address of the home page for a website in the URL window of your browser.

Hachette UK's policy is to use papers that are natural, renewable and recyclable products and made from wood grown in well-managed forests and other controlled sources. The logging and manufacturing processes are expected to conform to the environmental regulations of the country of origin.

Orders: please contact Hachette UK Distribution, Hely Hutchinson Centre, Milton Road, Didcot, Oxfordshire, OX11 7HH. Telephone: +44 (0)1235 827827. Email education@hachette.co.uk Lines are open from 9 a.m. to 5 p.m., Monday to Friday. You can also order through our website: www.hoddereducation.com

ISBN: 978 1398 30133 7

© John Reynolds 2021

First published in 2013

This edition published in 2021 by
Hodder Education,
An Hachette UK Company,
Carmelite House
50 Victoria Embankment
London EC4Y 0DZ

www.hoddereducation.com

Impression number    10 9 8 7 6 5 4 3 2 1

Year        2025 2024 2023 2022 2021

Typeset in FS Albert Light by DC Graphic Design Limited, Hextable, Kent.

Printed in UK

A catalogue record for this title is available from the British Library.

# Contents

# Introduction

Welcome to *Cambridge Checkpoint English Workbook Stage 7*. The chapters in this book complement the corresponding student's book and support the material contained in it. Each chapter contains text extracts with questions to test your understanding of both the content of the passages and your appreciation of the ways in which writers use language to create effects. Each chapter also contains exercises to allow you to practise a range of key skills to become fully competent in your ability to understand and write English.

There is no set way to approach using the workbook – you may wish to use it to supplement your understanding as you work through each chapter of the student's book or you may prefer to use it to recap on particular topics at a later point. It is hoped that the organisation of the material in the book is sufficiently flexible to allow whichever approach is best suited to your needs.

Please note: as the intention of this book is that it will be used by individual students to practise English activities away from the classroom and other students, there are no activities in the workbook that are aimed specifically at practising group work and discussion. Many of the reading passages and writing activities, however, contain ideas and topics that can be used as a basis for group discussions and talks to a small group, for students who wish to use the workbook for informal practice sessions with peers. There are opportunities to practise your listening and speaking skills – if you can perform your speaking tasks in front of an audience then you will get the most out of them.

There are also two extension activities – these are more demanding tasks or tasks that help you to practise a wider range of skills.

# It's a fact

## Reading

### Textbook text

The following passage is a piece of factual writing. Read it carefully and then answer the questions that follow.

> ## The Channel Tunnel
>
> Plans for an undersea tunnel joining Britain and France were first drawn up by a French engineer, Albert Mathieu, in 1802. The idea was to transport passengers by horse-drawn carriage. However, as hostilities developed between Britain and France, the idea was dropped.
>
> 5 Nevertheless, people still thought about the possibility throughout the nineteenth and twentieth centuries. After the invention of the railway, much thought was given to building a rail tunnel, but as early trains were pulled by steam-powered locomotives, there were significant practical problems with this idea, as well as the continuing fear that such a tunnel could be used for hostile invasions of both countries.
>
> In the early 1870s, however, the Channel Tunnel Company Ltd started to dig shafts for a tunnel but 10 the project was abandoned in 1875 when there was a change of UK government.
>
> A hundred years later, in the early 1970s, work started again but was abandoned for economic reasons. At last, in 1985, it was finally agreed that the project would go ahead but would be funded privately and not by taxpayers. Various proposals were put forward both for road and rail tunnels and for different types of bridges. The outcome was that a rail tunnel, to be built by the Channel Tunnel 15 Company, was chosen and construction began in 1988.
>
> The tunnel was to run from Folkestone in southeast England to Coquelles in northern France. There would be two rail tunnels plus a central service tunnel. The project involved over 1500 workers and the total cost was around £4650 million (about $7 billion).
>
> The two ends of the tunnel finally met in 1990 and the tunnel was completed and opened on 6 May 20 1994. It carries both high-speed passenger trains (London to Paris, Brussels and Amsterdam), shuttles for cars and passengers and freight. All are electrically powered. At 23.5 miles (37.5 kilometres) in length, the Chunnel, as it is known, is the longest undersea tunnel in the world.

Now answer these questions. You should try to use your own words in your answers as much as possible.

**1** Write down what you think the writer's purpose is in writing this text, and who their intended audience is. Say what evidence you have for your decision.

..............................................................................................................................................................

..............................................................................................................................................................

..............................................................................................................................................................

**2** Suggest a reason why a rail tunnel was thought to be impractical in the nineteenth century.

..............................................................................................................................................................

..............................................................................................................................................................

**3** How many tunnels were eventually constructed? ...................................................................................

**4  a** How has the writer organised this article? Find each topic sentence and compare them to help you map out the structure.

..............................................................................................................................................................

..............................................................................................................................................................

**b** Why do you think the writer has chosen to use this structure? Think about what the writer's purpose is in writing the text. Does this structure help them achieve it?

..............................................................................................................................................................

..............................................................................................................................................................

**5** State five facts given in the passage about the Channel Tunnel. **You should refer to the last three paragraphs only.**

**a** ...................................................................................................................................................

**b** ...................................................................................................................................................

**c** ...................................................................................................................................................

**d** ...................................................................................................................................................

**e** ...................................................................................................................................................

**6** Look at the numbers *nineteenth* and *twentieth*. The suffix '-th' has been added to turn the numbers in adjectives. Using the same patterns you can see in those words, turn the following numbers into adjectives:

**a** eighteen .............................................................................................................................

**b** eighty .................................................................................................................................

**c** eight ...................................................................................................................................

## Tourist guide text

Here is a piece of factual writing from the 'Hostelbookers' website. Read it carefully and then answer the questions that follow.

# How to travel on a limited budget

The words 'cheap travel' can conjure up nightmare images of unreliable tour packages and cowboy hoteliers. And, for the unwary, this could indeed become reality, but it really needn't be the case for travellers on a budget!

With a little forward planning, you will find that less can indeed be more in the world of cheap travel;
5  a bit of extra cash in your pocket can mean another week (or even two) of travels and adventures.

The number one rule when it comes to cheap travel is to do some homework and plan ahead. The biggest costs of travelling will be transport and accommodation, and it follows that this is also where the biggest savings can be made.

Booking in advance with budget airlines can save huge amounts, as can checking dates (and times)
10  around your preferred time of travel to find the cheapest; airlines adjust prices according to demand and a flexible schedule can be a great way to find a great deal.

Accommodation prices are also often subject to variation; particularly depending where you book. Websites such as 'Hostelbookers' allow travellers to compare hostel prices quickly and find the best value options for cheap travel. Moreover, there's no additional booking fee charged on the price of
15  a bed!

Hostels and cheap hotels can change their prices at any time so it can pay to book early, especially during the peak season. Conversely, prices can drop at the last minute, but usually only out of season.

However, there's more to cheap travel than booking and research from home. Once you're on foreign soil, the best bet is to find some local secrets, especially when it comes to eating and drinking. Don't
20  be afraid to ask friendly locals, other travellers or the staff at your hostel for tips.

Sticking to a budget on your travels needn't hamper your trip; in fact, it can be an advantage. Staying around the spots geared towards tourism (and paying for the guidebook's 'top' attractions) can mean missing out on a real, authentic taste of the country or city where you're travelling. And stepping off the beaten track to find those low prices can be both exciting and rewarding!

Now answer these questions. You should try to use your own words in your answers as much as possible.

**1 a** The writer has used several adjectives in the first sentence. List them here:

.......................................................................................................................................

**b** Write out the sentence with the adjectives removed. Make sure you amend your grammar to fit the new sentence.

.......................................................................................................................................

**c** Compare the two sentences. How do the adjectives help the writer make their point?

.......................................................................................................................................

.......................................................................................................................................

**2** According to the author, why should you use websites such as 'Hostelbookers'?

.......................................................................................................................................

.......................................................................................................................................

**3** Why do you think 'Hostelbookers' is mentioned by name in the article?

.......................................................................................................................................

**4** What three groups of people should be consulted for advice once you are in a foreign country?

**a** ...............................................................................................................................

**b** ...............................................................................................................................

**c** ...............................................................................................................................

**5** Explain what is meant by 'spots geared towards tourism'. Why should you avoid such spots?

.......................................................................................................................................

.......................................................................................................................................

**6** In the first column of the table, list the different pieces of advice given in the passage about how to travel cheaply. In the second column, state what can be gained by following these tips.

You should use only information given in the passage and answer using your own words. Try to list the points as concisely as possible. Continue on a separate piece of paper if you need to.

| Budget travel advice | Benefits |
| --- | --- |
| | |

**7** Compare the way the two passages 'The Channel Tunnel' and 'How to travel on a limited budget' set out to give information. In particular, you should consider the tone of the passages, the language used, the way the texts are structured and the audiences at which you think each was aimed. Remember to use references from each text to support your response.

........................................................................................................

........................................................................................................

........................................................................................................

........................................................................................................

........................................................................................................

........................................................................................................

........................................................................................................

# Key skills

## Parts of speech: nouns

1 Remind yourself of the definitions of these types of nouns:
   - common nouns: names that refer to general objects, places, people and animals
   - proper nouns: names of particular people, places or things, which are usually capitalised, such as London or Pluto
   - collective nouns: words referring to a collection of things taken as a whole, such as family, bunch or group
   - abstract nouns: nouns for ideas or for something that isn't concrete, such as love or fear

Identify each noun used in the following paragraph and write it in the correct column in the table below.

It was Thursday, a normal day at school. Rohan and Shivane were in their classroom waiting for English, their favourite lesson, to begin. It was the last lesson before the morning recess. The class were reading a novel entitled *Emil and the Detectives*, which they were all enjoying. It was full of suspense and excitement. The book was originally written in German and was set in Berlin, the capital city of the country. Rohan had been reading the book on the bus as he travelled to school that morning. He wanted to be a detective when he was an adult. He told Shivane of this ambition. She laughed and said that she liked the book because it told her about life and society in another country in an earlier time. She wanted to travel to Europe when she was older.

| Common nouns | Proper nouns | Collective nouns | Abstract nouns |
|---|---|---|---|
|  |  |  |  |

## Bias

A biased text is one that is unbalanced. Texts can be biased if they show only one side of an argument and ignore inconvenient facts.

A balanced text considers both sides of an argument equally, even if it gives an opinion in favour of one side or the other.

Compare these two passages. They are both written about the same football match.

### Pompeii Pompadours 4–0 Herculaneum Heroes

The impressive Pompeii has romped into the third round of the Vesuvius Cup after destroying an uninspiring Herculaneum.

After a fireball of a first goal from Claudia, Pompeii scored another with ease five minutes later. Herculaneum's Julius scored a comical own goal in the 52nd minute.

5   The Heroes' Augustus conceded a penalty after committing a disgraceful foul. Felix sent the penalty rocketing into the net.

### Pompeii Pompadours 4–0 Herculaneum Heroes

Pompeii has managed to edge into the third round of the Vesuvius Cup after a lucky day against Herculaneum.

After Claudia surprised everyone with a lucky tap, Herculaneum's goalie Lucia held her own well against a messy attack from Pompeii, and nearly held them off. Julius, usually fantastic, scored an

5   unfortunate own goal in the 52nd minute.

Pompeii's Felix took advantage of a penalty that he was lucky to be awarded after a tackle by Augustus.

**1** Each passage was written by a fan of one of the teams. Which team's fan wrote each article?

   **a** .................................................................................................................................................

   **b** .................................................................................................................................................

**2** Write a new, balanced article describing the events of the Pompeii vs Herculaneum match. Think about which word choices in particular show bias, and what descriptions you will need to change or remove completely.

.................................................................................................................................................

.................................................................................................................................................

.................................................................................................................................................

.................................................................................................................................................

7

## Paragraph structuring and linking

Here is an informative piece of writing consisting of five paragraphs about the Nile Delta in Egypt. You have been given the text of the first and last paragraphs; the topics of paragraphs 2, 3 and 4; and a list of points to be included in these paragraphs (labelled A–P).

The points are jumbled up and you will need to reorganise them into the correct order and write the letters into the table to indicate which points will appear in each paragraph.

Once you have sorted the points under paragraph headings you should then write your own version of the article, making sure that you include all points in the list. You may change or adapt the wording of the points and should focus on producing paragraphs that link with each other and in which the sentences are linked internally.

You should think about using appropriate connectives to link your paragraphs and points; you will find a list of the most frequently used connectives on page 36 of this workbook.

### Paragraph 1

The fertile region known as the Nile Delta has for thousands of years provided much of Egypt's food. Over 4000 years ago, the inhabitants of the area developed irrigation systems so that they could increase the area of land in which crops could be grown to support the population. Important crops such as beans, cotton, wheat and flax grew freely in the soil and could be stored easily.

Paragraph 2: The Nile in ancient times

Paragraph 3: The Nile in the present day

Paragraph 4: Problems and concerns

### Paragraph 5

The Nile River, nevertheless, remains an important trade route, which links Africa with markets in the rest of the Northern Hemisphere.

### Points to be included

**A** Ideal for growing papyrus

**B** Canals have been dug to bring its water to and from cities

**C** The richness of the soil of the Nile Delta comes from the river's deposits of silt and sediment

**D** This results in the Delta area shrinking as a result of erosion

**E** The river supports agriculture and fishing

**F** Dams have been built to make navigation easier

**G** The annual flooding of the Nile no longer occurs

**H** It continues to play an important role in transportation

**I** Dams, such as the Aswan High Dam also are used for hydroelectric power

**J** Inhabitants used the river's natural resources for their own purposes and to trade with others

**K** The water is now becoming increasingly polluted

**L** The building of the Aswan Dam has prevented this sediment flowing into the Delta area

**M** The river was also crucial for bathing, drinking and transportation

**N** Used for many purposes: cloth making, rope and most importantly paper

**O** The silt is now building up behind the Dam

**P** 95 per cent of Egyptians still live in close proximity to the Nile

| Paragraph 2 | Paragraph 3 | Paragraph 4 |
|---|---|---|
|  |  |  |

...............................................................................................................

...............................................................................................................

...............................................................................................................

...............................................................................................................

...............................................................................................................

...............................................................................................................

...............................................................................................................

...............................................................................................................

...............................................................................................................

# Writing

## Information leaflet

Write a one-page information leaflet for students joining your school. The leaflet's purpose is to help them in their first week at their new school and it should contain only **facts**. You should include information and advice about: times of the school day; getting around the school; what happens at break and lunch times; key school rules, and so on.

Consider what organisational features you could use to suit your chosen purpose, such as headings, bullet points and numbered lists.

Remember to adjust the tone and voice of your writing to suit the audience and think about which words will help to convey your message clearly.

Plan your work in the space below and then design your answer on a computer. Think carefully about how the layout of your leaflet will help to make the information on it clear and easy to read.

..................................................................................................................

..................................................................................................................

..................................................................................................................

..................................................................................................................

..................................................................................................................

..................................................................................................................

..................................................................................................................

..................................................................................................................

..................................................................................................................

..................................................................................................................

..................................................................................................................

..................................................................................................................

# 2 Growing up

## 🔊 Listening and reading

### Childhood memories

Mary Seacole was a Jamaican nurse who lived in the nineteenth century and spent much of her life in Europe, where she practised her medical skills. In particular she played a significant role in treating wounded soldiers during the Crimean War (1853–56) and became highly thought of in English society.

If you can access **www.hoddereducation.co.uk/cambridgeextras**, then listen to the audio of a passage taken from the opening pages of her autobiography. If you cannot access the audio then read the text below carefully and then answer the questions that follow.

---

## Extract: *The Adventures of Mary Seacole in Many Lands*

It is not my intention to dwell at any length upon the recollections of my childhood. My mother kept a boarding-house in Kingston, and was, like very many of the Creole women, an admirable doctress; in high repute with the officers of both services, and their wives, who were from time to time stationed at Kingston. It was very natural that I should inherit her tastes; and so I had from early youth a yearning
5  for medical knowledge and practice which has never deserted me.

When I was a very young child I was taken by an old lady, who brought me up in her household among her own grandchildren, and who could scarcely have shown me more kindness had I been one of them; indeed, I was so spoiled by my kind patroness that, but for being frequently with my mother, I might very likely have grown up idle and useless. But I saw so much of her, and of her
10  patients, that the ambition to become a doctress early took firm root in my mind; and I was very young when I began to make use of the little knowledge I had acquired from watching my mother, upon a great sufferer – my doll. I have noticed always what actors children are. If you leave one alone in a room, how soon it clears a little stage; and, making an audience out of a few chairs and stools, proceeds to act its childish griefs and blandishments upon its doll. So I also made good use of my
15  dumb companion; and whatever disease was most prevalent in Kingston, be sure my poor doll soon contracted it. I have had many medical triumphs in later days, and saved some valuable lives; but I really think that few have given me more real gratification than the rewarding glow of health which my fancy used to picture stealing over my patient's waxen face after long and precarious illness.

Mary Seacole

---

Now answer these questions. You should try to use your own words in your answers as much as possible.

1   Explain the meaning of the following words and phrases as used in the passage. In some cases, you have been given a related word or an etymological clue in brackets. In other cases, you will need to rely on the context of the sentence:

   **a** inherit her tastes .............................................................................................................................

   ....................................................................................................................................................................

   **b** yearning ...............................................................................................................................................

   ....................................................................................................................................................................

   **c** patroness ............................................................................................................................................

   ....................................................................................................................................................................

   **d** blandishments (the Latin word 'blandus' meant 'flattering') ...........................................

   ....................................................................................................................................................................

   **e** prevalent ('to prevail' means 'to win') ....................................................................................

   ....................................................................................................................................................................

2   According to paragraph 2 what did the writer gain from the old lady, and what problem might have developed from this?

   ....................................................................................................................................................................

   ....................................................................................................................................................................

3   On whom did the writer say she first practised her medical skills?

   ....................................................................................................................................................................

4   Explain, using your own words, the two sentences 'I have noticed always what actors … upon its doll.'

   ....................................................................................................................................................................

   ....................................................................................................................................................................

**5** In what ways did the writer extend her practice?

......................................................................................................................................................

**6** What evidence can you find in this passage that it was written over 150 years ago? In your answer you should refer closely to the details contained in the passage and the language used by the writer.

......................................................................................................................................................

......................................................................................................................................................

......................................................................................................................................................

......................................................................................................................................................

......................................................................................................................................................

......................................................................................................................................................

......................................................................................................................................................

......................................................................................................................................................

The next passage was written by the English poet and writer Laurie Lee (1914–97), who wrote two volumes of autobiography, *Cider with Rosie* and *As I Walked Out One Midsummer Morning*.

In the passage below he questions how far any autobiographical account of past experiences, such as details of childhood experiences, can ever be said to be actually true as the account is often slightly distorted by the writer's subsequent experiences. Read the passage carefully and then answer the questions that follow.

## Extract: *I Can't Stay Long*

Which brings me to the question of truth, of fact, often raised about autobiography. If dates are wrong, can the book still be true? If facts err, can feelings be false? One would prefer to have truth both in fact and feeling (if either could ever be proved). And yet … I remember recording some opinions held by my mother which she had announced during a family wedding. 'You got your mother

5 all wrong,' complained an aunt. 'That wasn't at Edie's wedding, it was Ethel's.'

Ours is a period of writing particularly devoted to facts, to a fondness for data rather than divination, as though to possess the exact measurements of the Taj Mahal is somehow to possess its spirit. I read in a magazine recently a profile of Chicago whose every line was a froth of statistics. It gave me a vivid picture, not so much of the city, but of the author cramped in the archives.

10 In writing autobiography, especially one that looks back at childhood, the only truth is what you remember. No one else who was there can agree with you because he has his own version of what he saw. He also holds to a personal truth of himself, based on an indefatigable self-regard. One neighbour's reaction, after reading my book, sums up this double vision: 'You hit off old Tom to the life,' he said. 'But why d'you tell all those lies about me?'

15 Seven brothers and sisters shared my early years, and we lived on top of each other. If they all had written of those days, each account would have been different, and each one true. We saw the same events at different heights, at different levels of mood and hunger – one suppressing an incident as too much to bear, another building it large around him, each reflecting one world according to the temper of his day, his age, the chance heat of his blood. Recalling it differently, as we were bound to

20 do, what was it, in fact, we saw?

Which one among us has the truth of it now? And which one shall be the judge? The truth is, of course, that there is no pure truth, only the moody accounts of witnesses.

But perhaps the widest pitfall in autobiography is the writer's censorship of self. Unconscious or deliberate, it often releases an image of one who could never have lived. Flat, shadowy, prim and

25 bloodless, it is a leaf pressed dry on the page, the surrogate chosen for public office so that the author might survive in secret.

Laurie Lee

Now answer these questions. You should try to use your own words in your answers as much as possible.

**1** Explain the meaning of the following words and phrases as used in the passage. In some cases, you have been given a related word or an etymological clue in brackets. In other cases, you will need to rely on the context of the sentence:

**a** If facts err, can feelings be false?

.......................................................................................................................

**b** divination (some people believe you can use a 'divining rod' to lead you to underground water)

.......................................................................................................................

**c** the author cramped in the archives

.......................................................................................................................

**d** indefatigable ('fatigue' is extreme tiredness or the feeling of being worn out)

.......................................................................................................................

**e** suppressing ('sup-' is another version of the prefix 'sub-', meaning 'down')

.......................................................................................................................

**2** What is the particular concern expressed by the writer in the first paragraph of the passage?

.......................................................................................................................

.......................................................................................................................

**3** What point is the author explaining by his reference to the 'exact measurements of the Taj Mahal'?

.......................................................................................................................

**4** How is this point further illustrated by the mention of the magazine article about Chicago?

.......................................................................................................................

**5** What reasons does the writer give for each of his brothers and sisters remembering the same event differently?

.......................................................................................................................................

.......................................................................................................................................

**6** By referring closely to the lines from 'The truth is, of course ...' (the last sentence of paragraph 5) to the end of the passage, explain **a)** why the writer thinks that 'there is no pure truth' and **b)** what he thinks about how authors of autobiographies portray themselves.

**a** .......................................................................................................................

**b** .......................................................................................................................

**7** Make a list of the main points made by the writer of this passage about the problems of writing autobiography. How far do you think that they are reflected in the 'Childhood' extract, written by Mary Seacole?

.......................................................................................................................................

.......................................................................................................................................

.......................................................................................................................................

.......................................................................................................................................

.......................................................................................................................................

**8** Based on the passages you have listened to and read here, which person would you like to read more about? Use examples from each passage to explain your preference.

.......................................................................................................................................

.......................................................................................................................................

.......................................................................................................................................

.......................................................................................................................................

.......................................................................................................................................

.......................................................................................................................................

.......................................................................................................................................

# Key skills

## Tenses, literary effects and annotation

This is a passage taken from an autobiographical essay by the poet Dylan Thomas in which he describes his childhood memories of bank holidays spent by the seaside in Wales. He uses many verb forms but not all of them are used to create a verb tense – many are used as adjectives or nouns.

Identify the verb forms in the passage. Underline any that are being used to create a verb tense. Then answer the questions that follow.

---

## Extract: *Quite Early One Morning*

August Bank Holiday – a tune on an ice-cream cornet. A slap of sea and a tickle of sand. A fanfare of sunshades opening. A wince and whinny of bathers dancing into deceptive water. A tuck of dresses. A rolling of trousers. A compromise of paddlers. A sunburn of girls and a lark of boys. A silent hullabaloo of balloons.

5   I remember the sea telling lies in a shell held to my ear for a whole harmonious, hollow minute by a small, wet girl in an enormous bathing suit marked Corporation Property.

I remember sharing the last of my moist buns with a boy and a lion. Tawny and savage, with cruel nails and rapacious mouth, the little boy tore and devoured. Wild as seedcake, ferocious as a hearthrug, the depressed and verminous lion nibbled like a mouse at his half a bun and hiccupped in
10  the sad dusk of his cage.

I remember a man like an alderman or a bailiff, bowlered and collarless, with a bag of monkeynuts in his hand, crying "Ride 'em, cowboy!" time and again as he whirled in his chairaplane giddily above the upturned laughing faces of the town girls bold as brass and the boys with padded shoulders and shoes sharp as knives; and the monkeynuts flew through the air like salty hail.

15  Children all day capered or squealed by the glazed or bashing sea, and the steam-organ wheezed its waltzes in the threadbare playground and the waste lot, where the dodgems dodged, behind the pickle factory.

And mothers loudly warned their proud pink daughters or sons to put that jellyfish down; and fathers spread newspapers over their faces; and sandfleas hopped on the picnic lettuce; and someone had
20  forgotten the salt.

In those always radiant, rainless, lazily rowdy and skyblue summers departed, I remember August Monday from the rising of the sun over the stained and royal town to the husky hushing of the roundabout music and the dowsing of the naphta jets in the seaside fair: from bubble-and-squeak to the last of the sandy sandwiches.

Dylan Thomas

---

1  What do you notice about the verb tenses in this passage? Complete the following table by underlining the verb and writing in the correct subject and tense.

| Verb | Subject | Tense (past/present/future/perfect) |
|---|---|---|
| I remember the sea telling lies in a shell held to my ear for a whole harmonious, hollow minute. | | |
| the little boy tore and devoured | | |
| I remember a man like an alderman or a bailiff, bowlered and collarless | | |
| I remember sharing the last of my moist buns with a boy and a lion. | | |
| and sandfleas hopped on the picnic lettuce | | |
| and someone had forgotten the salt | | |
| and the monkeynuts flew through the air like salty hail | | |

2  Identify:

   a  the tense in which the narrator is speaking

      past / present / future / perfect

   b  the tense in which the scenes he is describing are written

      past / present / future / perfect

   c  the effect of using two different tenses in the passage.

   ...................................................................................................................................

   ...................................................................................................................................

   ...................................................................................................................................

3  Look at how many times Thomas has used verb forms as adjectives and nouns. Why do you think he has used so many verb forms, rather than other types of adjectives and nouns?

   ...................................................................................................................................

   ...................................................................................................................................

   ...................................................................................................................................

   ...................................................................................................................................

**4** Annotate the extract by underlining literary effects you notice the writer using. Think particularly about the sounds and images the author is trying to create. You could consider:

– onomatopoeia (words that sound like the noise they describe)

– alliteration (words that begin with the same sound) and assonance (words that sound similar)

– rhyme, rhythm and repetition

– metaphor and simile.

Label at least three of your underlinings with a sentence or short note that explains what effect you think the author's choice has in that part of the passage.

**5** Now think about the passage's structure. You have already started thinking about this by looking at the way the author has used verbs, but now look at the other choices he has made about what order to write the events and descriptions in the text, and what length to make his paragraphs. Underline and label two structural choices in the passage.

**6** Now you have thought about the author's word choices and the literary effects and structure he has chosen to use, write down your thoughts about how these choices work together. Do you think the author has succeeded in creating the images and atmosphere he was hoping for? Why, or why not? Has the author created a distinctive voice? Use examples from the text to support your answer.

........................................................................................................................

........................................................................................................................

........................................................................................................................

........................................................................................................................

........................................................................................................................

**7** Identify the spelling rules used for the following words:

**a** sharing, rising, dowsing

........................................................................................................................

**b** hiccupped, hopped

........................................................................................................................

**c** devoured, warned, capered, squealed, upturned, whirled

........................................................................................................................

# Writing

## Remembering a family day out

Write an autobiographical account entitled 'A family day out' in which you describe a day when you and your family or caregivers went on a day out or a short trip, which you have a clear memory of. It could even be a description of a visit to another country or a holiday.

Your account should focus on your memories of what happened and what you and other members of your family did – think about the overall structure and how you will portray your sequence of events accurately – remember, you can use connectives to sequence and link ideas.

Consider what linguistic techniques you could use to enhance your writing and use a range of punctuation in your sentences and dialogue to vary your writing.

Plan your work in the space below and then write your answer on a separate piece of paper. Once you have finished, look at the activity at the bottom of the page.

# Handwriting

Look back at what you have just read. In general, are you pleased with your handwriting or are there things you would like to improve? It is important to feel comfortable when you are writing, and to write in a style that others can read!

In a new colour, circle or highlight any words or letters in your work which you think are difficult to read or you would prefer to look tidier.

Do you notice any letters or letter patterns which you often find difficult? Try practising writing these patterns a few times, or even changing the way you write them, until you feel more confident and you are happier with the way your writing looks and feels.

# 3 Painting with words

## Reading

### Describing places and people

The next two passages are examples of descriptive writing. The first is taken from the famous Sherlock Holmes mystery story *The Hound of the Baskervilles* and describes the interior of a rather gloomy house in a remote part of the English countryside. As you read it, you could consider how the description helps to set the scene for the mysterious events that follow later in the story.

The second is from the nineteenth-century novel *Vanity Fair* by W. M. Thackeray and introduces the comic (but also rather sad) character of Jos Sedley, a would-be fashionable young man who is both too old and too fat to be the type of character he would like to be.

Read this extract carefully and then answer the questions that follow.

---

### Extract: *The Hound of the Baskervilles*

A square balustraded gallery ran round the top of the old hall, approached by a double stair. From this central point two long corridors extended the whole length of the building, from which all the bedrooms opened. My own was in the same wing as Baskerville's and almost next door to it. These rooms appeared to be much more modern than the central part of the house, and the bright paper
5 and numerous candles did something to remove the sombre impression which our arrival had left upon my mind.

But the dining room which opened out of the hall was a place of shadow and gloom. It was a long chamber with a step separating the dais where the family sat from the lower portion reserved for their dependants. At one end a minstrel's gallery overlooked it. Black beams shot across above our heads,
10 with a smoke-darkened ceiling beyond them. With rows of flaring torches to light it up, and the colour and rude hilarity of an old-time banquet, it might have softened; but now, when two black-clothed gentlemen sat in the little circle of light thrown by a shaded lamp, one's voice became hushed and one's spirit subdued.

A dim line of ancestors, in every variety of dress, from the Elizabethan knight to the buck [trendsetter]
15 of the Regency, stared down upon us and daunted us by their silent company. We talked little, and I for one was glad when the meal was over and we were able to retire into the modern billiard room.

**************************************************************************************

I drew aside my curtains before I went to bed and looked out from my window. It opened upon the grassy space which lay in front of the hall door. Beyond, two copses of trees moaned and swung in a rising wind. A half moon broke through the rifts of racing clouds. In its cold light I saw beyond the
20 trees a broken fringe of rocks, and the long, low curve of the melancholy moor. I closed the curtain, feeling that my last impression was in keeping with the rest.

Sir Arthur Conan Doyle

Now answer these questions on the extract about Baskerville Hall. You should try to use your own words in your answers as much as possible.

1 Explain the meaning of the following words and phrases as used in the passage. In some cases, you have been given a related word or an etymological clue in brackets. In other cases, you will need to rely on the context of the sentence:

**a** balustraded .........................................................................................................................

..................................................................................................................................................

**b** sombre (the Latin 'umbra' means 'shade' and the 's' is a shortened prefix 'sub-')..........................

..................................................................................................................................................

**c** rude hilarity .........................................................................................................................

..................................................................................................................................................

**d** daunted ('dauntless' means 'brave') ....................................................................................

..................................................................................................................................................

**e** melancholy ............................................................................................................................

..................................................................................................................................................

2 Explain, using your own words, the layout of the dining room. ('It was a long chamber ... for their dependants.')

..................................................................................................................................................

..................................................................................................................................................

**3** Describe the behaviour of the writer and his companions while they were in the dining room.

..................................................................................................................................

**4** Why do you think that the diners 'talked little'?

..................................................................................................................................

..................................................................................................................................

**5** Explain, as fully as you can, what the writer means in the last sentence of the passage.

..................................................................................................................................

..................................................................................................................................

**6** This passage comes from the early stages of a mystery story. Referring closely to the writer's language and choice of words, explain how he creates an atmosphere of mystery and suspense.

..................................................................................................................................

..................................................................................................................................

..................................................................................................................................

..................................................................................................................................

..................................................................................................................................

..................................................................................................................................

..................................................................................................................................

..................................................................................................................................

..................................................................................................................................

..................................................................................................................................

In the next passage Jos Sedley has recently returned to London after a period of working in India, where he contracted a liver disease. Some of the language is explained for you. George 'Beau' Brummell (1778–1840) was a leading fashion icon (a 'dandy') of the Regency Period in England and a friend of King George IV. Read this extract carefully and then answer the questions that follow.

## Extract: *Vanity Fair*

Luckily, at this time he caught a liver complaint, for the cure of which he returned to Europe, and which was the source of great comfort and amusement to him in his native country. He did not live with his family while in London, but had lodgings of his own, like a gay young bachelor. Before he went to India he was too young to partake of the delightful pleasures of a man about town, and plunged into them
5   on his return with considerable assiduity. He drove his horses in the Park; he dined at the fashionable taverns (for the Oriental Club was not as yet invented); he frequented the theatres, as the mode was in those days, or made his appearance at the opera, laboriously attired in tights and a cocked hat.

On returning to India, and ever after, he used to talk of the pleasure of this period of his existence with great enthusiasm, and give you to understand that he and Brummell were the leading bucks
10  [trendsetters] of the day. But he was as lonely here as in his jungle at Boggley Wollah. He scarcely knew a single soul in the metropolis: and were it not for his doctor, and the society of his blue-pill, and his liver complaint, he must have died of loneliness. He was lazy, peevish, and a *bon-vivant* [someone who lives well]; the appearance of a lady frightened him beyond measure; hence it was but seldom that he joined the paternal circle in Russell Square, where there was plenty of gaiety, and where
15  the jokes of his good-natured old father frightened his *amour-propre* [self-esteem]. His bulk caused Joseph much anxious thought and alarm; now and then he would make a desperate attempt to get rid of his superabundant fat; but his indolence and love of good living speedily got the better of these endeavours at reform, and he found himself again at his three meals a day. He never was well dressed; but he took the hugest pains to adorn his big person, and passed many hours daily in that occupation.
20  His valet [servant] made a fortune out of his wardrobe [collection of clothes]: his toilet-table was covered with as many pomatums [dressings for the hair] and essences as ever were employed by an old beauty: he had tried, in order to give himself a waist, every girth, stay, and waistband then invented. Like most fat men, he *would* have his clothes made too tight, and took care they should be of the most brilliant colours and youthful cut. When dressed at length, in the afternoon, he would
25  issue forth to take a drive with nobody in the Park; and then would come back in order to dress again and go and dine with nobody at the Piazza Coffee-House. He was as vain as a girl; and perhaps his extreme shyness was one of the results of his extreme vanity.

W. M. Thackeray

**1** Look at the first sentence. What effect does the word 'luckily' have on the sentence it opens?

.................................................................................................................................................

**2** The writer uses three similes in this extract to build detail and help the reader picture Jos.

  **a** What simile does the author use in the first paragraph to show us how Jos wants to present himself?

.................................................................................................................................................

  **b** What similes does the author use in the second paragraph to tell us what Jos is really like?

.................................................................................................................................................

.................................................................................................................................................

**3** What does the word 'laboriously' in line 7 suggest about Jos's way of dressing?

........................................................................................................................

**4** Look at the opening sentence of the second paragraph.

   **a** The independent clause in this sentence is 'he used to talk.' Find the dependent clause that tells you what Jos used to talk about, and how he would talk?

   ........................................................................................................................

   **b** You can identify the dependent clauses in the sentence by looking for the connectives. Explain what each of these new details tells us about Jos:

   **On** returning to India

   ........................................................................................................................

   **and** ever after

   ........................................................................................................................

   **and** give you to understand that he and Brummell were the leading bucks of the day

   ........................................................................................................................

**5** Identify the connective (used as a sentence opener) which splits the extract into two, and say what effect using this connective and this structure has on the way the reader understands Jos.

........................................................................................................................

**6** What do you think is the writer's true opinion of Jos Sedley? Does he think he is a fool? Is he laughing at him? Does he show any sympathy towards him? Explain your comments as fully as you can and refer closely to the passage in your answer.

........................................................................................................................

........................................................................................................................

........................................................................................................................

........................................................................................................................

........................................................................................................................

# Key skills

## Semi-colons and punctuating for clarity

Semi-colons can be used make lists clearer, or to link two independent clauses:

The shop is closed; I will have to buy milk tomorrow.

**1** Rewrite the above sentence with an appropriate connective:

..................................................................................................................................

**2** Now rewrite it with a full stop:

..................................................................................................................................

**3** Compare the sentences. What is the effect of using a semi-colon?

..................................................................................................................................

**4** Add a semi-colon to these sentences in the appropriate place:

**a** In summer I play cricket in winter I do athletics.

..................................................................................................................................

**b** My friend likes history I prefer maths.

..................................................................................................................................

**c** One day I'm going to visit America I want to see the Statue of Liberty.

..................................................................................................................................

**d** She is really good at using semi-colons her sister is less sure.

..................................................................................................................................

**5** Now think about these sentences. Punctuate them to make sense, using any punctuation you think is appropriate. There may be more than one correct answer!

**a** adil is wearing a sky blue jumper henrys is sea green

..................................................................................................................................

**b** when I finish school I'm going to my grandmothers my mum will still be at work

..................................................................................................................................

**c** let me see if I can find it the librarian said I had asked if they had my favourite book

..................................................................................................................................

## Returning to prepositions

Prepositions are words that tell you where something is in relation to something else. They are commonly used words with which all speakers of English are familiar. They are very important in allowing writers to express their meaning precisely but it is easy to misuse them, and teachers point out that one of the most common mistakes students make in their writing is to misuse prepositions.

Read the pairs of sentences below and then explain as fully as you can the difference in the meaning of the prepositions indicated in each pair.

**1** During break time we all talked <u>about</u> the concert we had been to the night before.

When we came to school this morning, we had a lecture <u>on</u> the importance of healthy eating from a visiting speaker.

.......................................................................................................................

.......................................................................................................................

**2** The trip was very tiring as we spent a long time making our way <u>through</u> the dense forest.

Once we had left the forest we had to paddle <u>across</u> a river in canoes.

.......................................................................................................................

.......................................................................................................................

**3** At the end of the first day of the trip the teacher produced a tin of sweets that we shared <u>among</u> ourselves.

We passed some time that evening comparing the differences <u>between</u> the forest walk and the canoe trip across the river.

.......................................................................................................................

.......................................................................................................................

**4** My best friend has an identical twin and I often confuse her <u>with</u> my friend.

I read through the instructions for my maths homework and was very confused <u>about</u> how to make a start on it.

.......................................................................................................................

.......................................................................................................................

## How writers build up detail

The passage that follows is taken from the opening pages of Charles Dickens's *A Christmas Carol*, published in 1843. In this extract he describes Ebenezer Scrooge, a rich and bad-tempered miser.

Read through the passage carefully and then answer the question that follows.

### Extract: *A Christmas Carol*

Oh! But he was a tight-fisted hand at the grindstone, Scrooge! a squeezing, wrenching, grasping, scraping, clutching, covetous, old sinner! Hard and sharp as flint, from which no steel had ever struck out generous fire; secret, and self-contained, and solitary as an oyster. The cold within him froze his old features, nipped his pointed nose, shrivelled his cheek, stiffened his gait; made his eyes red, his thin lips
5 blue; and spoke out shrewdly in his grating voice. A frosty rime was on his head, and on his eyebrows, and his wiry chin. He carried his own low temperature always about with him; he iced his office in the dog-days; and didn't thaw it one degree at Christmas.

External heat and cold had little influence on Scrooge. No warmth could warm, no wintry weather chill him. No wind that blew was bitterer than he, no falling snow was more intent upon its purpose,
10 no pelting rain less open to entreaty. Foul weather didn't know where to have him. The heaviest rain, and snow, and hail, and sleet, could boast of the advantage over him in only one respect. They often "came down" handsomely, and Scrooge never did.

Nobody ever stopped him in the street to say, with gladsome looks, 'My dear Scrooge, how are you? When will you come to see me?' No beggars implored him to bestow a trifle, no children asked him
15 what it was o'clock, no man or woman ever once in all his life inquired the way to such and such a place, of Scrooge. Even the blind men's dogs appeared to know him; and when they saw him coming on, would tug their owners into doorways and up courts; and then would wag their tails as though they said, 'No eye at all is better than an evil eye, dark master!'

But what did Scrooge care! It was the very thing he liked. To edge his way along the crowded paths
20 of life, warning all human sympathy to keep its distance, was what the knowing ones call 'nuts' to Scrooge.

Charles Dickens

Explain as fully as you can the impression you gain of the narrator's voice from reading this passage.

Look closely at how Dickens uses connectives and adjectives to build the picture, and how he chooses to open his sentences. Are there any ways of writing which stand out to you?

You could also start looking at how Dickens varies the length of his sentences. What effect do you think he is trying to achieve when he uses short sentences? What about when he uses long ones?

Plan your answer in the space below and write it down on a separate piece of paper. Make sure you write down your own opinion of the description of Scrooge, using examples from the text to support your point. Do you think it is an effective description? Why, or why not?

.............................................................................................................................................................

.............................................................................................................................................................

.............................................................................................................................................................

.............................................................................................................................................................

## Choosing the right word

Read the descriptive passage below carefully and try to build up a clear picture in your mind of the scene being described.

Write out the passage choosing the best words from the options given. Think about what literary effects you would like to create: are you trying to help the reader imagine a sound, or a visual effect? Do any of the words create different feelings or moods? There are no absolutely correct answers – the important thing is that you consider the choices carefully in order to produce a consistent and convincing description.

> The sky (*frowned/glared/sulked*) over the town. In the streets pedestrians (*quaking/shaking/shivering*) in the wind and driving rain (*dragged/stumbled/trudged*) past shops. Cars (*crawled/dawdled/plodded*) along the road, their drivers (*blinking/squinting/staring*) as their windscreen wipers (*clunked/knocked/thudded*) monotonously. It had been raining (*ceaselessly/consistently/solidly*) for three hours and
> 5  the water (*gurgled/splashed/spluttered*) as it (*flowed/ran/streamed*) from the gutters onto the (*overflowing/teeming/gushing*) sidewalk. The only relief from the (*deluge/downpour/storm*) could be found within the Percolator Coffee House, whose (*civil/sympathetic/welcoming*) interior offered (*animation/solace/warmth*) and comfort.

...................................................................................................................................................................

...................................................................................................................................................................

...................................................................................................................................................................

...................................................................................................................................................................

...................................................................................................................................................................

...................................................................................................................................................................

...................................................................................................................................................................

...................................................................................................................................................................

...................................................................................................................................................................

...................................................................................................................................................................

...................................................................................................................................................................

# Writing

## Describing a shop

Write a description of your favourite local shop and of some of the people who work in it. Try to capture the sights, sounds and overall atmosphere of the place.

Think about your words carefully and try to be as accurate as possible in the description you give. Use a range of sentence types to build up detail. Remember you can make use of pronouns and use connectives to link and compare ideas. Plan your work in the space below and then write your answer on a separate piece of paper.

## Reading

### Facts and opinions

The two texts in this chapter are non-fiction accounts – the first outlines the life of the famous author Roald Dahl while the second is a newspaper article about food miles. Although both of these examples consist mainly of factual details, when reading them you should also think about how much the personal opinions of the writers become apparent.

First read the passage below about Roald Dahl and answer the questions that follow.

## Roald Dahl

Roald Dahl's parents were from Norway, but he was born in Wales on 13 September 1916. The family used to spend the summer holidays on a little Norwegian island, swimming, fishing and going by boat. When Roald was four years old, his father died, so his mother had to organise the trip alone for herself and her six children.

5　After school, Roald Dahl didn't go to university, but applied for a job at the Shell Company, because he was sure they would send him abroad. He was sent to East Africa, where he got the adventure he wanted: great heat, crocodiles, snakes and safaris. He lived in the jungle, learned to speak Swahili and suffered from malaria. When the Second World War broke out, he went to Nairobi to join the Royal Air Force. He was a fighter pilot and shot down German planes but got shot down himself. After six
10　months in hospital he flew again.

In 1942, he went to Washington as Assistant Air Attaché [a post in the British Embassy]. There, he started writing short stories. His collections of short stories have been translated into many languages and have been best-sellers all over the world. He wrote TV series like *Tales of the Unexpected* and the novel *My Uncle Oswald*.

15　His books are mostly fantasy, and full of imagination. They are always a little cruel, but never without humour – a thrilling mixture of the grotesque and comic.

Roald Dahl didn't only write books for grown-ups, but also for children, such as *James and the Giant Peach*, *Fantastic Mr Fox* and *The Gremlins*. About his children's stories he said once: 'I make my points by exaggerating wildly. That's the only way to get through to children.' Roald Dahl is perhaps the most
20　popular and best-selling children's book author. However, these stories are so sarcastic and humorous that adults also appreciate reading them.

Roald Dahl died on 23 November 1990. *The Times* newspaper called him 'one of the most widely read and influential writers of our generation'.

Now answer these questions. You should try to use your own words in your answers as much as possible.

1   From the information given in paragraph 2, what conclusions can you make about Roald Dahl's character and interests?

......................................................................................................................................

......................................................................................................................................

......................................................................................................................................

2   What do you think makes Roald Dahl's books for adults particularly appealing to readers? (You should refer to the passage in your answer.)

......................................................................................................................................

......................................................................................................................................

......................................................................................................................................

3   What was Roald Dahl's trick for making his stories interesting for young readers?

......................................................................................................................................

......................................................................................................................................

4   Why, according to the writer, are Roald Dahl's books for children enjoyed by adults as well?

......................................................................................................................................

......................................................................................................................................

5   This is a non-fiction piece of writing; however, it is not entirely factual. Write down all the opinions that it contains.

......................................................................................................................................

......................................................................................................................................

......................................................................................................................................

6   Do the descriptions of Roald Dahl's writing make you want to read any of his books? Which ones would you be tempted by, and why? Are there any which you would want to avoid? Why, or why not?

......................................................................................................................................

Now read the article about food miles below, and then answer the questions that follow.

# What are food miles?

Have you ever thought where your food comes from? In this special report, we take a closer look at our everyday groceries to find out exactly where they are grown. You might be surprised at just how far they travel!

*The further your food travels, the more greenhouse gases are emitted*

### Food miles explained

The idea of food miles is really simple – the clue is in the name! Food miles refers to the distance that our food has travelled to get from the place where it was grown, to landing on our plates in the UK. Although this might sound like an easy thing to calculate, it's actually rather tricky.

Food passes from the farmer to a processor, distributor and retailer, and often makes multiple journeys back and forth between these different people. Our food travels more than we ever could; sometimes a product might make a round-the-world expedition before it arrives in our freezers! We consume faraway foods from a wide variety of places on a daily basis, racking up an incredible number of food miles every year. For example, bananas take 4,560 miles (7,340km) to get from Jamaica to London, and prawns can travel a mighty 7,306 miles (11,760km) from Indonesia!

### Why are food miles important?

Food miles are a useful way to judge how much impact we have on the environment. Food and packaging is transported in lorries, boats and aeroplanes. These forms of transport run on fossil fuels, like petrol and diesel. When these fuels are burned, they release gases that contribute to global climate change. Transporting food around the UK represents nearly 25% of all journeys made by lorries, which also run on fossil fuels.

### Why do we import foods from abroad?

While it's easy to suggest that we should always buy foods that are grown or raised locally, sometimes it's just not that simple. An important study carried out by DEFRA, the Government department in charge of food and farming, claims that it is more environmentally friendly to grow and transport tomatoes from Spain than it is to produce them locally in the UK. That's because it needs a lot of electricity to heat up greenhouses in milder British weather. In other cases, buying certain foods from poorer countries will create lots of food miles but might help develop the economy of those countries. That's not to say that we should stop trying to be responsible shoppers. Food miles force us to question where our food actually comes from, so we might make better choices when we visit the shops.

### What can you do to help?

Eating fresh fruit and vegetables that are not covered in packaging – which adds an often unnecessary stage to food production – is an important step. Farmers' markets sell food when it is in season, so it does not need to be imported from warmer countries – so it's a good idea to shop at these markets, or to visit a local farm or garden centre that allows you to pick your own for a small price when their crops are in season.

The best way to reduce your food miles impact is to grow some of your fruit and vegetables yourself. Think seasonally and sow

seeds in advance so they're ready for picking in the right months.

Before tucking in on your next meal, have a think about what exciting places your food might have come from!

**1** This report has several structural elements that are often found in articles. Label and explain the purpose of the:

**a** headline ....................................................................................................................

**b** introduction ..............................................................................................................

**c** subheadings .............................................................................................................

**d** conclusion ................................................................................................................

**2** Do you think the article is balanced? Use examples to support your answer.

........................................................................................................................................

........................................................................................................................................

........................................................................................................................................

**3** Explain in your own words what you think the purpose of the article is. Does it aim to persuade the reader? If so, what does it persuade the reader to do? Use examples to support your answer.

........................................................................................................................................

........................................................................................................................................

**4** Find and write down four examples of emotive language from the article, or language which expresses an opinion, rather than a fact. How does it affect the reader?

........................................................................................................................................

........................................................................................................................................

........................................................................................................................................

........................................................................................................................................

**5** Do you think the article is successful? How do you feel about food miles now you have read it?

.......................................................................................................................................

.......................................................................................................................................

.......................................................................................................................................

.......................................................................................................................................

**6** Do you think the article is designed in a way that would tempt you to read it? Think about what changes you might make if you wanted to make the article grab your friends' attention and make them more likely to read it.

.......................................................................................................................................

.......................................................................................................................................

.......................................................................................................................................

**7** Find as many words as you can in the article that begin with the prefixes 'in-' or 'im-'. Describe the spelling rule and write a sentence containing each word.

.......................................................................................................................................

.......................................................................................................................................

.......................................................................................................................................

.......................................................................................................................................

.......................................................................................................................................

**8** These words are all taken from the article. Write down another word from the same family and explain the meanings of both:

**a** incredible ...................................................................................................................

**b** unnecessary .................................................................................................................

**c** imported .....................................................................................................................

# Key skills

## Connectives

Connectives are words or phrases that link the different components of a piece of writing (clauses, sentences, paragraphs) in order to contribute to a cohesive whole. Connectives may be simple conjunctions (such as *and, when, because*) or connecting adverbs or adverbial clauses or phrases (such as *however, on the other hand, as revealed by*). Choosing connectives thoughtfully is a key to producing a convincing and logically ordered piece of writing.

Here is a list of the most common connectives and the purposes for which they are used:
- **to support or add:** and, moreover, also, as well as, besides, furthermore, similarly
- **to show order or sequence:** next, then, first, second, third, …., finally, eventually, after, before
- **to contrast:** but, whereas, instead of, alternatively, otherwise, unlike, on the other hand, however, although, except, unless, if, as long as
- **to show cause and effect:** because, so, therefore, thus, consequently
- **to illustrate:** for example, such as, for instance, as revealed by, in the case of.

The passage below is adapted from a book written in 1915 called *Chess Strategy*. It is about the mistakes beginners often make when they are learning to play the game. Read it carefully and then, on a separate piece of paper, list the connectives it uses. For each one, explain how it ties the information together to help the reader understand the advice.

## Extract: *Chess Strategy*

The development of the chess player is a gradual struggle from a state of chaos to a clear understanding of the game. The time required for this development largely depends upon the special gifts the learner may possess, but, to begin with, the understanding of strategy is important.

Most beginners do not follow a particular plan in their study of chess, yet as soon as they have learnt
5  the moves, rush into playing games. It is obvious that their prospects therefore cannot be very bright. The play of a beginner is often planless, because they have too many plans, let alone the ability to cut down all the combinations to one leading idea. Still, it cannot be denied that a certain kind of method is to be found in the play of all beginners, and seems to come to them quite naturally.

First, the pawns are pushed forward frantically because there is no appreciation of the power and
10  value of the pieces. The beginner is often concerned with attacking the opposing pieces with their pawns in the hope of capturing them, even though it can be advantageous to use the greater power of the pieces. The beginner's aim is not to develop their own forces but to weaken those of their opponent. Their combinations are made in the hope that their challenger may not see through them. Moreover, beginners often don't think too much about their opponent's intentions.

15  Many beginners also have a great liking for the Queen and the Knight – the Queen because of her tremendous mobility and the Knight because of his peculiar step, which seems particularly suited to take the enemy by surprise as a result. When watching beginners, you will frequently see meandering moves by a roaming Queen and reckless attacks into the enemy's camp by a Knight. Furthermore, when the other pieces join in, combinations of moves follow in bewildering sequence and fantastic
20  chaos. This unsteadiness in the first stages of development makes it very difficult for the beginner to get a general view of the board, yet the surprises which each move brings give them great enjoyment.

A few dozen such games are by no means wasted. After certain moves have proved their undoing, the beginner will become aware of threats and traps. They will start to see danger one or two moves ahead, consequently reaching the second stage in their development.

https://www.gutenberg.org/files/5614/5614-h/5614-h.htm

## Apostrophes

**1** Add apostrophes in the correct place in the following sentences:

   **a** I bought these from the mens clothes shop.

   **b** The childrens play area is out of bounds.

   **c** Im afraid hes busy on Wednesday.

   **d** The museum doesnt open until eleven o clock.

   **e** His friend wasnt at home.

   **f** This potatos mine, thats yours, and those potatoes are hers.

   **g** 'Its a beautiful day,' thought the boy, as he watched the bird fly up to its nest.

**2** Use possessive apostrophes to shorten these sentences.

   **a** The party for Mia was excellent.

   ..........................................................................................................................

   **b** The rainfall for June was unusually high.

   ..........................................................................................................................

   **c** The section for children in the library closes at three.

   ..........................................................................................................................

   **d** The capital city of France is Paris.

   ..........................................................................................................................

**3** Explain in your own words why a writer might want to use the shorter or longer version of one of the sentences above.

..........................................................................................................................

..........................................................................................................................

..........................................................................................................................

**4** Look at the following sentences. Explain the difference in meanings between the sentences.

   **a** I'm visiting my auntie's house tomorrow.

   I'm visiting my aunties' house tomorrow.

   ......................................................................................................................................................

   ......................................................................................................................................................

   **b** The cats played around the girl's feet

   The cats played around the girls' feet.

   ......................................................................................................................................................

   ......................................................................................................................................................

   **c** I bought these from the men's clothes shop.

   I bought these from the man's clothes shop.

   ......................................................................................................................................................

   ......................................................................................................................................................

   **d** The boy's books were on the shelf.

   The boys' books were on the shelf.

   ......................................................................................................................................................

   ......................................................................................................................................................

## Fact or opinion?

One thing to consider when you are reading a piece of factual writing is whether or not everything that looks like fact actually is a fact. Is it a fact that can be proved or is the writer presenting opinion as fact in order to make their argument sound more convincing?

For example:
- 'In the 2018 soccer World Cup Final, France beat Croatia by 4–2.' This is a **fact** as there is plenty of evidence (television recordings, newspaper reports, and so on) that this is true.
- 'The French team that won the World Cup in 2018 is the greatest soccer team of all time.' This is an **opinion** as it is not possible to prove that this team was better than any other side that has ever played soccer.
- 'Statements made by many experts confirm that the French World Cup winners of 2018 were the greatest soccer team there has ever been.' You need to think about this one. The language introducing the comment makes it sound as if it is a fact, but all it is really stating is that many experts have **said this**. It is still not possible to prove that this was the greatest ever team and so the point remains the experts' **opinion**.

Read the following statements. Decide whether each one is fact or opinion and then write **F** (for fact) or **O** (for opinion) in the boxes.

1  Nelson Mandela was appointed as President of South Africa on 10 May 1994. ☐

2  The Amazon is the longest river in South America. ☐

3  Basketball is the most exciting sport of all. ☐

4  It is understood that eating an apple a day keeps you healthy. ☐

5  *Titanic* won the Best Film Oscar in 1997. ☐

6  Leonardo di Caprio was undoubtedly the star performer in *Titanic*. ☐

7  The square root of 144 is 12. ☐

8  In time, scientists will be able to prove how the universe was formed. ☐

9  Life on Earth would not exist without water. ☐

10 Many scholars have said that *Hamlet* is the greatest play written by Shakespeare. ☐

## Building detail in sentences

Verb phrases are phrases you can use in the place of single-word verbs.

**1** Compare the sentences. Underline the verb phrases and, in your own words, explain what they change about the meaning of the sentences:

**a** He ate the ice cream.

He must have eaten the ice cream.

........................................................................................................................................

........................................................................................................................................

**b** Darina moves to Kiev soon.

Darina must be moving to Kiev soon.

........................................................................................................................................

........................................................................................................................................

**c** George's aunt ran a restaurant in Sydney.

George's aunt used to run a restaurant in Sydney.

........................................................................................................................................

........................................................................................................................................

You can also build detail in sentences by using connectives and punctuation to add more clauses. The more clauses you add, the more you have to think about what order to put them in and what connectives will work best.

**2** Compare these sentences, and in your own words, explain what change has been made (for example, from a simple sentence to a complex sentence) and what effect it has:

**a** The cat was small. It had sharp teeth.

The cat was small, but it had sharp teeth.

........................................................................................................................................

........................................................................................................................................

**b** I eat a lot. I play a lot of sport. Sport makes me hungry.

Because I play a lot of sport and it makes me hungry, I eat a lot.

.....................................................................................................................

.....................................................................................................................

**c** The woods were deserted. The trees rustled in the breeze. Anjali shivered.

The trees rustled in the breeze in the deserted woods; Anjali shivered.

.....................................................................................................................

.....................................................................................................................

**d** The museum was closed. Jason checked his watch.

The museum, which should have opened at nine, was closed, so Jason checked his watch.

.....................................................................................................................

.....................................................................................................................

**3** Expand these sentences to make them more descriptive. There are no right answers but think about what techniques you know to add more information about the nouns and verbs. How can you tell your readers more?

**a** The door to the house was open.

.....................................................................................................................

.....................................................................................................................

**b** The ladder was leaning against the wall.

.....................................................................................................................

.....................................................................................................................

**c** Brian didn't want to go to school.

.....................................................................................................................

.....................................................................................................................

**4** Now read this extract.

> Dodos have always been a famous symbol of an extinct species. The bird was sadly hunted to extinction within a few decades of European settlement on the island of Mauritius. They were unfortunately saddled with two difficulties that made them easy to catch and quick to die out when humans (and vermin from the ships) arrived: they were completely flightless, and they are now
> 5 thought to have only laid clutches of one egg at a time. To the poor Dodo, flightlessness would have obviously been a sensible adaptation for its surroundings, as it would surely have had very few natural predators until the explorers made their sudden entrance in Mauritius.

Comment on how the writer has built up detail with the use of verb phrases and different sentence types. What do these choices add to the passage that might be lacking without them?

..................................................................................................................................................

..................................................................................................................................................

..................................................................................................................................................

..................................................................................................................................................

..................................................................................................................................................

..................................................................................................................................................

..................................................................................................................................................

..................................................................................................................................................

..................................................................................................................................................

..................................................................................................................................................

..................................................................................................................................................

..................................................................................................................................................

..................................................................................................................................................

# Writing

## Writing to influence and persuade

Think of an endangered animal about which you have strong feelings. Write a newspaper or magazine article that makes a powerful appeal to people in your age group in order to make them aware of your concerns.

Think about what literary and linguistic techniques might enhance your writing. Also consider the structure and organisation of your writing and how this will help you with your intended purpose of raising awareness. Think carefully about:
- how you will start each paragraph and sentence to have maximum impact
- how you might sequence your ideas with connectives
- how you can build detail in your sentences using verb phrases and a variety of sentence types.

Plan your work in the space below and then use a computer to write your answer. Include an image and consider the layout and subject line or title carefully to create the maximum impact on your reader. Look at articles on the internet or in a newspaper for ideas.

When you have finished your piece, read it through carefully and evaluate the language, grammar, layout and structure you have used. Would your piece influence and persuade your peers about your important issue?

..........................................................................................................................................

..........................................................................................................................................

..........................................................................................................................................

..........................................................................................................................................

..........................................................................................................................................

..........................................................................................................................................

..........................................................................................................................................

..........................................................................................................................................

..........................................................................................................................................

..........................................................................................................................................

..........................................................................................................................................

## Formal and informal letters

You recently left an item (for example, a book, musical instrument, piece of sports equipment) on the bus on your way home from school. Write two letters:

**a** a formal letter, using standard English, to the bus company describing the item, giving details of when and where it was lost and asking for information about where to collect it if it has been found

**b** a letter or email to your cousin who lives in a different town describing what happened after you discovered that you had lost the item.

Make sure that you include all necessary addresses, and so on, and that the greeting and ending of each letter is appropriate for the person to whom it will be sent. You should pay particular attention to the tone you use for each letter – the one to your cousin is likely to be much more familiar.

Plan your work in the space below and then write your letters on a separate piece of paper or on the computer. If you have written your letters by hand, look back at your handwriting to make sure it is clear and easy to read.

## Reading

### Fables

A fable is a type of folk tale that contains a moral or a lesson for the reader. Here is a fable by the Greek storyteller Aesop, who lived about 2500 years ago. The moral still holds true today.

Read the fable carefully and then answer the questions that follow.

---

## 'The Man, the Boy and the Donkey'

A man and his son were once going with their donkey to market. As they were walking along by its side a countryman passed them and said: 'You fools, what is a donkey for but to ride upon?'

So the man put the boy on the donkey and they went on their way. But soon they passed a group of men, one of whom said: 'See that lazy youngster, he lets his father walk while he rides.'

5 So the man ordered his boy to get off, and got on himself. But they hadn't gone far when they passed two women, one of whom said to the other: 'Shame on that lazy lout to let his poor little son trudge along.'

Well, the man didn't know what to do, but at last he took his boy up before him on the donkey. By this time they had come to the town, and the passers-by began to jeer and point at them. The man
10 stopped and asked what they were scoffing at. The men said: 'Aren't you ashamed of yourself for overloading that poor donkey of yours with yourself and your hulking son?'

The man and boy got off and tried to think what to do. They thought and they thought, till at last they cut down a pole, tied the donkey's feet to it, and raised the pole and the donkey to their shoulders. They went along amid the laughter of all who met them till they came to Market Bridge,
15 when the donkey, getting one of his feet loose, kicked out and caused the boy to drop his end of the pole.

In the struggle the donkey fell over the bridge, and his fore-feet being tied together, he was drowned.

'That will teach you,' said an old man who had followed them.

---

Now answer these questions. You should try to use your own words in your answers as much as possible.

1 Practise reading this folk tale aloud. Think particularly about:
   – reading ahead, especially to plan for the different speakers
   – how fast and loud you speak
   – how often you pause
   – how you make it clear when a new character is speaking.

If you can, record yourself or ask someone to listen to you. Listen carefully to your recording and write down one thing that you did well, and three improvements you would like to make next time.

..........................................................................................................................................

..........................................................................................................................................

..........................................................................................................................................

..........................................................................................................................................

2 Explain, using your own words, what the women's criticism of the father was.

..........................................................................................................................................

..........................................................................................................................................

3 What did the group of men in the town accuse the father and son of doing?

..........................................................................................................................................

..........................................................................................................................................

4 How did the man, the boy and the donkey finally arrive at Market Bridge and what happened after they reached it?

..........................................................................................................................................

..........................................................................................................................................

..........................................................................................................................................

**5** Explain, as fully as you can, what you think the moral of this story is.

..................................................................................................................................

..................................................................................................................................

..................................................................................................................................

..................................................................................................................................

..................................................................................................................................

The next story is a modern retelling of a traditional folk tale from India. Read it carefully and then answer the questions that follow.

## 'King of the Birds'

The birds of the jungle had no king. It was a real embarrassment for them since everyone else in the jungle had a king.

A king is someone who heads the flock and decides everything for them. All the birds decided they too needed a king. They called a meeting to resolve the problem.

5 But who would be the king?

The Mynah bird had an idea. 'Let the bird who can fly the highest be made king of the air,' she said.

One of the birds, Eagle, was a braggart. He was big and strong, and was sure that he would win.

He strutted around, and asked: 'Why not make me king now? You know I can fly the highest.'

'Still, you may not win,' piped a little voice. Eagle turned to see who had said that. It was Sparrow.
10 'Oh!' he said in a mocking voice. 'And who's going to beat me? You?' he asked, letting out a loud, crackling laugh.

The little birds, the middle-sized birds and the big birds all got ready for the race. It was decided that Owl should start the race. When everyone was ready, Owl cried, 'Whoo, whoo!'

As soon as Owl signalled, all the birds took to the air.

15 Up, up, up they went, far into the blue sky.

But they could not fly very high and very fast for long. One by one, they dropped out of the race. Only Eagle went on flying, as strong as ever. 'High, high … I'm a bird in the sky … I'm an eagle that flies so high,' he sang. At length, he looked below him and saw that all the birds had given up.

'Oh! What did I say!' he exclaimed. 'I am king of the air and all the birds that fly.'

20 What Eagle did not know was that tiny Sparrow had been flying under his wing. The moment he stopped, Sparrow darted out. He flew just above Eagle's head and cried out, 'No, no, no, Mr Eagle. I'm king of the birds. Look, I've flown higher than you.'

All the birds agreed with Sparrow. In any case, they were glad to see proud Eagle beaten. He had boasted too much. So they chose Sparrow as their king.

25 Eagle did not like this at all. He could not bear to see the crown being placed on Sparrow's head. So he caught the little bird in his claws and threw him to the ground.

Although Sparrow did not get hurt, he found that Eagle had torn away half his tail. 'Oh well! I'll still be king,' he told himself.

And ever since, Sparrow has had a short tail.

Brishti Bandyopadhyay

Now answer these questions. You should try to use your own words in your answers as much as possible.

1 Explain the meaning of the following words and phrases as used in the passage. In some cases, you have been given a related word or an etymological clue in brackets. In other cases, you will need to rely on the context of the sentence:

a real embarrassment ...........

b resolve the problem ('dissolve' and 'solve' are both related to 'resolve')...........

c braggart ('to brag' means 'to boast')...........

d strutted ...........

e mocking ...........

f exclaimed (a 'clamour' is a loud noise made by people shouting)...........

**2** The words 'piped' and 'loud, crackling' are used in the story to describe sounds the birds make. How do these words help you to understand the characters of Sparrow and Eagle?

..........................................................................................................................

..........................................................................................................................

..........................................................................................................................

**3** Explain fully, using your own words, how Sparrow managed to fly higher than Eagle.

..........................................................................................................................

..........................................................................................................................

**4** By referring closely to the passage, list as many differences as you can between Sparrow and Eagle.

..........................................................................................................................

..........................................................................................................................

**5** Explain, as fully as you can, what you think the moral is of this story. (You may consider that there is more than one moral; if so, explain them all.)

..........................................................................................................................

..........................................................................................................................

..........................................................................................................................

..........................................................................................................................

..........................................................................................................................

..........................................................................................................................

# Key skills

## Hyphens – revision and practice

We use hyphens to link words together to make sentences clearer. They are mostly used to create compound adjectives by linking two or more words together to make one adjective. For example:
— She pulled on her **well-worn** boots and stepped outside.
— The dog looked up at him with his **chestnut-brown** eyes.

There are exceptions. Some compound adjectives don't take hyphens – you can just combine the whole word into one – and sometimes you can use '-ly' instead of a hyphen:
— He had an expensive, formal jacket and an **everyday** coat.
— This is a **highly paid** job.

You don't usually need to hyphenate or combine compound adjectives that come after the noun:
— Her boots were **well worn**.
— His dog's eyes are **chestnut brown**.
— He wore his brown coat **every day**.

Sometimes hyphens are used after a prefix to make the meaning of a word clearer if another, similar word exists:
— The librarian **re-covered** (put a new cover on) a book.
— The librarian **recovered** (found) a book.

**1** Describe the difference in meaning between these phrases, depending on how hyphens have been used:

   **a** He wore his blue-collared shirt.

     He wore his blue collared shirt.

     .................................................................................................................................................

     .................................................................................................................................................

   **b** DANGER: MAN EATING SHARK

     DANGER: MAN-EATING SHARK

     .................................................................................................................................................

     .................................................................................................................................................

   **c** She had an appointment with the small-business manager.

     She had an appointment with the small business manager.

     .................................................................................................................................................

     .................................................................................................................................................

**d** I resent the email.

I re-sent the email.

........................................................................................................

........................................................................................................

**e** She taught a class of twenty-five-year-olds.

She taught a class of twenty five-year-olds.

She taught a class of twenty-five year-olds.

........................................................................................................

........................................................................................................

........................................................................................................

**2** Look at the sentences below and decide which sentence in each pair needs a hyphen. Add the hyphens as required:

**a** We decided to stop off at the service station.

We had a stop off at the service station.

**b** There was a break in at the shop overnight.

The owner had to break in by smashing a window.

**c** He loves rock climbing.

He is a rock climbing fan.

**3** Now put the hyphens in the correct places in these sentences:

**a** Mo had just moved into a new two bedroomed house with his twenty year old sister.

**b** Delilah needed to check out of the hotel before the official check out time.

**c** Justin read through his poorly worded essay and decided to make some carefully thought through changes.

**d** I bought my new hiking boots in a hiking boot sale.

## Punctuation: direct speech

Rewrite the passage below, adding speech marks in the correct places. It is quite tricky. You will probably need to read through the passage several times to work out what each character is saying. Again, remember the rule – new speaker, new line.

> Excuse me asked the stranger. Can you tell me where the library is? I'm not entirely sure because I'm a visitor here myself replied Anna. However, I went there with my friend a few days ago and I think it's very near the police station. The police station! exclaimed the stranger. That's good; I need to go there as well. Can you tell me how I get there from here? I think so said Anna. It's along the road
> 5 after the railway station. She pointed up the road. You turn left at the next junction and then it's on your left. Thanks said the stranger, looking confused but which place will I be at then? Oh, sorry said Anna. That's the railway station. Go past there, cross the road and turn right and the police station is opposite you. I'm sure the library is a bit further down the same road. Thanks a lot said the man. You've been very helpful.

# Writing

## A modern version of a folk tale

Research traditional folk tales, either in a library or on the internet. When you have found one whose moral appeals to you, write your own updated version of the story, setting it within the world with which you are familiar. Think about the overall structure of your tale and how you will portray your sequence of events clearly. Use a range of sentences to enhance your writing and build up detail and, remember, you can use connectives to compare, contrast, sequence and link ideas.

Plan your work in the space below and then write your story on a separate piece of paper.

Write down up to five words from your story which you found difficult to spell. Choose a strategy to help you remember the spellings – you might try making up a mnemonic, or thinking about other words from the same family. Challenge yourself to return to your spellings after a day to remember them.

# 6    Tell me a (short) story

## Reading

### Short story techniques

This chapter looks at a complete contemporary short story by the American writer Mike Krath. The story is divided into two parts with questions following each part. These questions will test your understanding of what happens in the story and also help you to consider the techniques used by the storyteller.

Chapter 7 also asks you to look at another short story: a traditional ghost story from Ukraine. At the end of this second story, you will find a question that asks you to write about both these stories in greater detail (see page 70).

Chapter 7 also asks you to look at another short story: a traditional ghost story from Ukraine. At the end of this second story, you will find a question that asks you to write about both these stories in greater detail (see page 70).

Here is the first part of Mike Krath's story. Read it carefully and then answer the questions that follow this first part.

---

## 'High and Lifted Up' – Part 1

It was a windy day.

The mailman barely made it to the front door. When the door opened, Mrs Pennington said, 'Hello', but, before she had a real chance to say 'thank you', the mail blew out of the mailman's hands, into the house, and the front door slammed in his face. Mrs Pennington ran to pick up the mail.

5    'Oh my,' she said.

Tommy was watching the shutters open and then shut, open and then shut.

'Mom,' he said, 'may I go outside?'

'Be careful,' she said. 'It's so windy today.'

Tommy crawled down from the window-seat and ran to the door. He opened it with a bang. The wind
10    blew fiercely and snatched the newly recovered mail from Mrs Pennington's hands and blew it even further into the house.

'Oh my,' she said again. Tommy ran outside and the door slammed shut.

Outside, yellow, gold, and red leaves were leaping from swaying trees, landing on the roof, jumping off the roof, and then chasing one another down the street in tiny whirlwinds of merriment.

15    Tommy watched in fascination.

'If I was a leaf, I would fly clear across the world,' Tommy thought and then ran out into the yard among the swirl of colours.

Mrs Pennington came to the front porch.

'Tommy, I have your jacket. Please put it on.'

---

20  However, there was no Tommy in the front yard.

'Tommy?'

Tommy was a leaf. He was blowing down the street with the rest of his playmates.

A maple leaf came close by, touched him and moved ahead. Tommy met him shortly, brushed against him, and moved further ahead. They swirled around and around, hit cars and poles, flew up into the
25  air and then down again.

'This is fun,' Tommy thought.

Mike Krath

Now answer these questions. You should try to use your own words in your answers as much as possible.

**1** Why did the mailman only 'barely' make it to the front door?

.......................................................................................................................................................

.......................................................................................................................................................

.......................................................................................................................................................

**2** Note down the verbs used by the writer in the paragraph beginning 'Outside, yellow, gold …' and comment on how the choice of these words helps to bring the scene alive.

.......................................................................................................................................................

.......................................................................................................................................................

.......................................................................................................................................................

.......................................................................................................................................................

**3** Explain what you think Tommy was feeling when he was outside in the yard. You should refer to the passage to support your answer.

.......................................................................................................................................................

.......................................................................................................................................................

.......................................................................................................................................................

.......................................................................................................................................................

**4** What have you learned about Mrs Pennington from this section of the story?

..............................................................................................................................

..............................................................................................................................

..............................................................................................................................

**5** Are you tempted to read the next part of the story? Why, or why not? Use examples from the text to support your answer.

..............................................................................................................................

..............................................................................................................................

..............................................................................................................................

..............................................................................................................................

**6** What would make a reader choose one story over another? List three things that you think would make someone want to read a particular story.

..............................................................................................................................

..............................................................................................................................

..............................................................................................................................

..............................................................................................................................

..............................................................................................................................

..............................................................................................................................

..............................................................................................................................

..............................................................................................................................

Next read carefully the second part of the story and then answer the questions that follow.

## 'High and Lifted Up' – Part 2

The maple leaf blew in front of him. It was bright red with well defined veins. The sunlight shone through it giving it a brilliance never before seen by a little boy's eyes.

'Where do you think we are going?' Tommy asked the leaf.

'Does it matter?' the leaf replied. 'Have fun. Life is short.'

5 'I beg to differ,' an older leaf said suddenly coming beside them. 'The journey may be short, but the end is the beginning.'

Tommy pondered this, the best a leaf could ponder.

'Where do we end up?'

'If the wind blows you in that direction,' the old leaf said, 'you will end up in the city dump.'

10 'I don't want that,' Tommy said.

'If you are blown in that direction, you will fly high into the air and see things that no leaf has seen before.'

'Follow me to the city dump,' the maple leaf said. 'Most of my friends are there.'

The wind blew Tommy and the maple leaf along. Tommy thought of his choices. He wanted to
15 continue to play.

'Okay,' Tommy said, 'I will go with you to the dump.'

The winds shifted and Tommy and the leaf were blown in the direction of the city dump.

The old leaf didn't follow. He was blown further down the block and suddenly lifted up high into the air.

'Hey,' he called out, 'the sights up here. They are spectacular. Come and see.'

20 Tommy and the maple leaf ignored him.

'I see something. I see the dump,' the old leaf cried out. 'I see smoke. Come up here. I see fire.'

'I see nothing,' the maple leaf said.

Tommy saw the fence that surrounded the city dump. He was happy to be with his friend. They would have fun in the dump.

25 Suddenly, a car pulled up. It was Tommy's mom. Mrs Pennington wasn't about to let her little boy run into the city dump.

'Not so fast,' she said getting out of the car. 'You are not allowed to play in there. Don't you see the smoke?'

Tommy watched the maple leaf blow against the wall and struggle to get over. He ran over to get it
30 but was unable to reach it.

Mrs Pennington walked over and took the leaf. She put it in her pocket.

'There,' she said, 'it will be safe until we get home.'

Tommy smiled, ran to the car and got in. He rolled down the back window and looked up into the sky. He wondered where the old leaf had gone. Perhaps one day he would see what the old leaf had seen –
35 perhaps.

Mike Krath

Now answer these questions. You should try to use your own words in your answers as much as possible.

1 Explain the meaning of the following words and phrases as used in the passage. In some cases, you have been given a related word or an etymological clue in brackets. In other cases, you will need to rely on the context of the sentence:

**a** well defined veins ......................................................................................................................

......................................................................................................................

**b** brilliance ......................................................................................................................

......................................................................................................................

**c** ponder ......................................................................................................................

......................................................................................................................

**d** spectacular (the Latin word 'specere' meant 'to look') ......................................................

......................................................................................................................

2 How does the old leaf's point of view differ from that of the maple leaf?

......................................................................................................................

......................................................................................................................

3 Why do you think Tommy should have listened to the old leaf and not ignored him?

......................................................................................................................

......................................................................................................................

4 Looking back at the story as a whole, do you think Tommy really turned into a leaf? Give reasons for your answer.

......................................................................................................................

......................................................................................................................

......................................................................................................................

**5** What point do you think the writer is making by presenting Tommy with the views of the old leaf and the maple leaf? What do you think Tommy has learned by the end of the story? Try to explain your response to the story as fully as you can and use references from the text.

..................................................................................................................

..................................................................................................................

..................................................................................................................

..................................................................................................................

..................................................................................................................

..................................................................................................................

..................................................................................................................

..................................................................................................................

**6** Look closely at the extract and highlight features that stand out to you. Think about:
- **structure:** What happens when? Who speaks in what order and why? When does the reader learn new information?
- **language:** What specific word choices does the writer make? Why do certain characters speak the way they do? Do any words or phrases stand out? Is any punctuation unusually effective?
- **literary features:** Is there any interesting imagery? Does the writer make any use of similes, metaphors or onomatopoeia?

What effect do you think the writer is hoping to achieve by using these features? Do you think he achieves it? Why, or why not? Use examples from the extract to support your answer, which you can write on a separate piece of paper.

# Key skills

## Multiple meanings: combine your skills

Some words mean different things depending on the context of the sentences around them. Use the context clues from the sentences in the table below to place the right words from the box in the gaps. Each pair of sentences will use the same word, but you may need to adjust the word to use the correct form – think about verb tenses and agreements. Once you have decided on which word to use, write a synonym or definition in the right-hand column. (If you have used the word as a proper noun or as a scientific term, it may already be the most useful term.)

| desert | minute | depress | refuse | entrance |
|---|---|---|---|---|

| | Synonym |
|---|---|
| 1 a Hari was _____ about his exam results.<br><br>b Please _____ the button to open the door. | |
| 2 a The Gobi _____ is the largest in Asia.<br><br>b The silent village in the middle of the forest had been _____ by its inhabitants long ago. | |
| 3 a Bake the cake for 30 _____ at 180°C.<br><br>b The watchmender had to use a magnifying glass to check the _____, detailed workings of the timepiece. | |
| 4 a The disposal service came to collect _____ once a week.<br><br>b The stubborn boy _____ to follow the rules. | |
| 5 a The audience were _____ by the mesmerising performance.<br><br>b You will find reception inside the main _____. | |

## Identifying figurative language

Read the following passage from 'The Five Orange Pips', a short story from *The Adventures of Sherlock Holmes* by Arthur Conan Doyle.

> ## Extract: *The Five Orange Pips*
>
> It was in the latter days of September, and the equinoctial* gales had set in with exceptional violence. All day the wind had screamed and the rain had beaten against the windows, so that even here in the heart of great, hand-made London we were forced to raise our minds for the instant from the routine of life and to recognise the presence of those great elemental forces which shriek at mankind through
> 5 the bars of his civilisation, like untamed beasts in a cage. As evening drew in, the storm grew higher and louder, and the wind cried and sobbed like a child in the chimney. Sherlock Holmes sat moodily at one side of the fireplace cross-indexing his records of crime, while I at the other was deep in one of Clark Russell's fine sea-stories until the howl of the gale from without seemed to blend with the text, and the splash of the rain to lengthen out into the long swash of the sea waves. My wife was on a visit
> 10 to her mother's, and for a few days I was a dweller once more in my old quarters at Baker Street.
>
> 'Why,' said I, glancing up at my companion, 'that was surely the bell. Who could come to-night? Some friend of yours, perhaps?'
>
> 'Except yourself I have none,' he answered. 'I do not encourage visitors.'
>
> 'A client, then?'
>
> 15 'If so, it is a serious case. Nothing less would bring a man out on such a day and at such an hour. But I take it that it is more likely to be some crony of the landlady's.'
>
> Sherlock Holmes was wrong in his conjecture, however, for there came a step in the passage and a tapping at the door. He stretched out his long arm to turn the lamp away from himself and towards the vacant chair upon which a newcomer must sit.
>
> 20 'Come in!' said he.
>
> Arthur Conan Doyle

*equinoctial *means happening at the time of the equinox, which is when the sun crosses the equator, so day and night are of equal length.*

**1** Find and highlight:

  **a** two examples of personification

  **b** one example of alliteration and one example of sibilance

  **c** one example of onomatopoeia

  **d** one example of a metaphor or a simile.

**2** This passage, at the beginning of the short story, is setting up the rising action. Identify the setting, the narration and who you think the protagonists and antagonists might be. Then, discuss how the figurative language you have identified creates suspense.

# Writing

## Narrative and informal writing

Write the following parts of two different short stories:

**a** the opening to a story containing mysterious happenings

**b** the conclusion to a story dealing with events in the life of a happy and contented family.

In both pieces of writing you should concentrate on conveying the atmosphere through your descriptions and choose your language precisely and accurately. Use a range of punctuation, such as ellipses, colons, semi-colons, dashes, hyphens, exclamation marks and brackets to help clarify your meaning. You should include **one character only** in each piece of writing.

Do **not** write complete stories.

**c** Imagine that you were present at one of the events of either (a) or (b) above. Write a letter to a close friend saying what happened and describing your feelings during this experience.

Plan your work in the space below and then write your story parts on a separate piece of paper. Think about the structures of all three pieces and how this will help you convey your intended purpose of each one.

## Reading

### A traditional short story

This chapter is based on a retelling of a traditional ghost story from Ukraine. The story has been divided into two parts with questions at the end of each part.

Read the first part of the story carefully and then answer the questions that follow. Try not to read to the end of the story before you have answered the questions on Part 1.

---

## 'Cow's Head' – Part 1

Oksana lived in a small house on the edge of town with her father, her stepmother and her stepsister. Oksana's stepmother disliked Oksana, favouring her true daughter, Olena.

Soon after her father's remarriage, Oksana found that all the housework fell to her while Olena idled her days away. Oksana's father was a timid man, and could not bring himself to defy his wife. So
5  Oksana wore Olena's cast-off clothes, and her hands grew red and chapped from scrubbing in the cold, while Olena attended parties, growing lazy and spoiled.

One year, when the winter snows were particularly fierce, Oksana's family ran out of money. Oksana's stepmother began nagging her father to send Oksana away, because they could not afford to keep two girls. Reluctantly, Oksana's father agreed. He took Oksana to a cottage deep in the woods and left
10  her there.

Oksana was very frightened. The woods were said to be filled with demons and monsters. But Oksana was also practical. She entered the cottage with her small bundle and found a fireplace, a lopsided table and a rusty old pot. Oksana put away the loaf of bread, the knife and the slab of cheese her father had given her. She folded the blanket and laid it near the fireplace. Then she collected wood
15  and built a fire.

Oksana knew the bread and cheese would not last her all winter. So she made a snare using the thin, flexible branches of the trees and caught a snow rabbit to eat. She also dug under the deep snow, and found some roots and berries for food.

By dark, Oksana had melted snow for drinking water, and used the rest to make a stew. So Oksana ate
20  well. Then she lay down near the fire for the night, listening to the wind howl and pretending to herself that she was not frightened of the woods.

Retold by S. E. Schlosser

Now answer these questions. You should try to use your own words in your answers as much as possible.

**1** Explain the relationships between Oksana and Olena, and Oksana's father and his new wife. Use references from the text.

.......................................................................................................................................

.......................................................................................................................................

.......................................................................................................................................

.......................................................................................................................................

.......................................................................................................................................

.......................................................................................................................................

.......................................................................................................................................

.......................................................................................................................................

.......................................................................................................................................

.......................................................................................................................................

.......................................................................................................................................

.......................................................................................................................................

**2** State one household chore that was done by Oksana.

.......................................................................................................................................

**3** What is meant by 'Oksana was also practical', and how did Oksana show this when she was in the cottage in the woods?

.......................................................................................................................................

.......................................................................................................................................

.......................................................................................................................................

**4** How did Oksana feed herself while she was in the woods?

..........................................................................................................................................

..........................................................................................................................................

..........................................................................................................................................

**5** What was Oksana frightened of and how did she try to overcome this?

..........................................................................................................................................

..........................................................................................................................................

..........................................................................................................................................

**6** **Before** you read Part 2 of the story, using clues from the passage, write down two or three events that you think will happen next in the story.

..........................................................................................................................................

..........................................................................................................................................

..........................................................................................................................................

..........................................................................................................................................

..........................................................................................................................................

..........................................................................................................................................

Read the second part of the story carefully and then answer the questions that follow.

## 'Cow's Head' – Part 2

It was midnight when the knock came.

Knock, knock, knock.

It echoed hollowly through the dark cottage. Oksana woke with a start, her heart pounding in fear. It came again.

5   Knock, knock, knock.

Oksana thought of the monsters. She hid under her blanket, praying the thing would go away.

Knock, knock, knock.

Oksana rose, grabbing a branch. She crept towards the door. The wind howled eerily down the chimney. Oksana swallowed and swung the door open. There was nothing there. Her heart pounded

10   fiercely as she stared out at the snow whipping about in the light of her small fire. Then she looked down. Oksana let out a shriek of terror and leapt back, dropping her stick. It was a demon. An evil spirit.

It had no body!

'Who are you?' Oksana stuttered, clutching the door with shaking hands.

'I am Cow's Head,' it replied.

15   Indeed, Oksana saw at once that it was. The head was brown, with curved horns and strange, haunted eyes.

'I am cold and hungry. May I sleep by your fire?' Cow's Head asked. Its voice was cold and lifeless.

Oksana gulped down her horror.

'Of course,' she said.

20   'Lift me over the threshold,' demanded Cow's Head hollowly. Oksana did as she was bidden.

'Place me near the fire.'

Anger warred with compassion inside her, but compassion won. Oksana put it next to the fire.

'I am hungry,' said Cow's Head. 'Feed me.'

Oksana thought of her meagre food supply. The stew left in the pot was for her breakfast. She fed it
25 to Cow's Head.

'I will sleep now,' it said. There was no softening in its attitude toward her. Nonetheless, Oksana made
it comfortable for the night, giving it her blanket and sleeping in a cold corner with only her cloak to
keep her warm.

When she woke in the morning, Cow's Head was gone. Where it had slept was a large trunk, filled with
30 the most beautiful gowns she had ever seen. Under the gowns lay heaps of gold and jewels.

Oksana stared blankly at the riches in front of her. Her father's voice roused her.

'Daughter, I am come.'

Oksana forgot the trunk in her joy. She ran into his arms. He had defied her stepmother to come and
bring her back to their home.

35 'Papa, come see!' Oksana exclaimed as she pulled him into the cottage. Her words tumbled over each
other as she explained.

Her father took her home. She was honoured in her town for her compassion and her bravery, and won
scores of suitors. She married soon after her return from the cottage.

Hearing Oksana's story, and seeing the riches she had received, Olena went to the cottage in the
40 forest and spent the night there. But when Cow's Head appeared, she was too lazy to serve it. In the
morning, all her gowns had turned to rags and her possessions to dust.

But Oksana lived to a ripe old age in happiness and prosperity.

Retold by S. E. Schlosser

Now answer these questions. You should try to use your own words in your answers as much as possible.

**1** Explain the meaning of the following words and phrases as used in the passage:

    **a** hollowly ...................................................................................................................................

    **b** eerily .......................................................................................................................................

    **c** the snow whipping about in the light of her small fire ...............................................

       .................................................................................................................................................

    **d** gulped down her horror ......................................................................................................

**2** At the beginning of Part 2 of the story, there are several one-line paragraphs. What effect does the writer achieve by using these?

.................................................................................................................................................

**3** What impression do the words 'cold and lifeless' and 'hollowly' give you of Cow's Head and the way in which it talks?

.................................................................................................................................................

.................................................................................................................................................

.................................................................................................................................................

.................................................................................................................................................

.................................................................................................................................................

.................................................................................................................................................

**4** What does the sentence 'Anger warred with compassion inside her, but compassion won' tell you about Oksana's state of mind?

.................................................................................................................................................

.................................................................................................................................................

**5** Which word tells you that Oksana had very little food to eat?

.................................................................................................................................................

**6** By referring closely to the conclusion of the story (from the paragraph beginning 'When she woke in the morning …' to the end), explain, as fully as you can, what has happened to Oksana, Olena and Oksana's father and how their characters have changed by the end of the story.

.......................................................................................................................................

.......................................................................................................................................

.......................................................................................................................................

.......................................................................................................................................

.......................................................................................................................................

.......................................................................................................................................

.......................................................................................................................................

**7** Think of someone who might like this story. Write down three things you would tell them about the story to encourage them to read it:

.......................................................................................................................................

.......................................................................................................................................

.......................................................................................................................................

.......................................................................................................................................

.......................................................................................................................................

The questions you have answered about 'Cow's Head' have tested your understanding of what happens in the story and also helped you to consider the techniques used by the storyteller. If you have already read and answered the questions about the story 'High and Lifted Up' in Chapter 6 (pages 54–59), you could now try the extension activity on the next page, which asks you to write about both stories in greater detail.

## Extension activity: identifying writing techniques; comparing two stories

Write a detailed comparison of the two stories 'High and Lifted Up' and 'Cow's Head'. In particular you should write about:

– the characters in the stories
– the descriptions of the background and weather
– how the writers use language, figurative language and structure for effect
– who you think the audiences for them are
– the endings of each story and the lessons each one contains for the reader.

In your conclusion say which of the stories you enjoyed more and give reasons for your choice.

Plan your work in the space below and then write your answer on a separate piece of paper.

.......................................................................................................................................................

.......................................................................................................................................................

.......................................................................................................................................................

.......................................................................................................................................................

.......................................................................................................................................................

.......................................................................................................................................................

.......................................................................................................................................................

.......................................................................................................................................................

.......................................................................................................................................................

.......................................................................................................................................................

.......................................................................................................................................................

.......................................................................................................................................................

.......................................................................................................................................................

.......................................................................................................................................................

.......................................................................................................................................................

# Key skills

## Deconstructing words

Using the given linked words and an etymology clue, can you work out the meanings of these words?

| Word | Linked words clue | Etymology clue | Meaning |
|---|---|---|---|
| halitosis | inhale, exhale | -*osis* is a scientific suffix that means 'condition of' or 'disease' | |
| detract | contract, retract, abstract, distract, attract, tractor | *trahere* is a Latin word that means 'to pull' or 'to draw' | |
| matriarchy | maternal, matrimony, maternity | *arkheia* is an ancient Greek word meaning 'leadership' | |
| monochrome | monotone, monorail, monopoly, monocle, monologue, monarchy | *khroma* is an ancient Greek word meaning 'colour' | |

# Writing

## A short story opening

Choose a place you know well (or the country you live in if you are stuck) and think about a national event, traditional game/sport or a significant period of history for your chosen place (for example, the Rio Carnival is a famous national event in Brazil and sumo wrestling is a traditional sport from Japan). Use this as a setting or focal point and write the opening of a short story. Try to convey the cultural practices of your chosen setting in detail for your readers – consider the customs and traditions of the country and the beliefs, knowledge and behaviours of your characters.

Think about the literary devices that have been used to good effect in the examples we have read, such as: alliteration, personification, similes and rhetorical questions.

To make your vocabulary more precise and imaginative for your readers, use a thesaurus and choose synonyms for words that are quite basic, for example you could write 'she *sprinted* away from the spaceship' instead of 'she *ran* away from the spaceship'.

When you have finished, check your spellings in a dictionary and check that you have used punctuation accurately.

# 8    Poems aplenty

## Reading

### Comparing poems

This chapter looks at two different types of poem. The first two examples are lyrical poems on a similar topic, both of which provide food for thought. These two poems are also dramatic as they are both written as the direct speech of an imagined character.

Read the first two poems carefully and then answer the questions that follow the second one. Some of the words and phrases in the first poem have been explained for you.

---

## Important Notice

World Wildlife Industries sadly announces
that we may soon have to close due to fierce
competition from Human Beings International.

5  Many of our famous products are already
unavailable including, to name but three, our *dodo*,
*quagga* and once healthy *passenger pigeon* lines.

> The dodo and passenger pigeon are extinct types of bird; quaggas were an ancient type of zebra, now also extinct.

Currently under threat are many of our
stock of mammals and fishes as well as
birds, reptiles, amphibians *and* insects.

10  But even now we could be helped to survive.
Work together with your parents and teachers
to find out how you could all help before it is too late.

And remember – without us and the products
of our other branch, World Vegetation Industries,
15  our world too might soon be without *your* company.

Let's work together to stay in business.

Mother Nature
Managing Director

Philip Waddell

---

# The Last Wolf Speaks from the Zoo

By day
I hid in the ferns
pressed to the earth,
dressed in a coat
5  brown as turf.

Sunlight warmed
the patches where
my wolf pack once lay.

Day after day
10  childflesh spills past the wire;
they pause, point and stare –
I size them up –
glare back –
through thin red eyes.

15  Years back
my sister caught one –
cracked a finger –
left the childflesh
to scowl and howl.

20  The next day
they took my sister away.
But her smell stayed
trapped in the earth's spoor.
It took a full moon's span
25  for it to fade.

Now, alone,
I watch
and wait for her.

At night
30  the stars glisten.
I listen for the pack.
I sing to the moon.
I croon an ancient tune.
But she is muzzled
35  and cannot answer back.

Pie Corbett

Now answer these questions on 'Important Notice' and 'The Last Wolf Speaks from the Zoo'. You should try to use your own words as far as possible.

**1** Explain, as fully as you can, what is being said in the opening three lines of 'Important Notice'. Who is speaking and what does the speaker represent?

..................................................................................................................................

..................................................................................................................................

..................................................................................................................................

..................................................................................................................................

..................................................................................................................................

..................................................................................................................................

**2** What is implied by the statement 'Many of our famous products are already unavailable'?

..................................................................................................................................

..................................................................................................................................

**3** What or who has caused this unavailability? How are readers of the poem being asked to help?

..................................................................................................................................

..................................................................................................................................

..................................................................................................................................

**4** Annotate the poem with your thoughts on its structure and language. Think about:

  **a** How many stanzas the poem has, and whether variations in their length affect the way you read or understand the poem.

  **b** How the poem is punctuated: are there any places where an established pattern is changed? What effect does this have?

  **c** Whether any particular words or phrases stand out to you, or take you by surprise. What effect is the poet trying to create by using them?

**5** In the second poem, where is the wolf and what is it referring to in the first eight lines of the poem?

......................................................................................................................

......................................................................................................................

**6** Explain as fully as you can the thoughts and memories the wolf refers to in the final verses of the poem (from 'But her smell ...').

......................................................................................................................

......................................................................................................................

......................................................................................................................

......................................................................................................................

......................................................................................................................

**7** Read this poem aloud to yourself, in order to help you find out whether it has any rhymes or rhythmic patterns. Pay close attention to stanza breaks and punctuation (including **enjambment**, where sentences flow onto the next line, and pausing for longer at dashes and semicolons). Annotate the poem with your thoughts.

**a** If you noticed any rhymes or assonance, what effect do they have?

**b** If you found any rhythms (or breaks in rhythm), how do they affect your understanding of that part of the poem?

## Extension activity: writing to analyse, review, comment; comparing two poems

Both of these poems contain a similar message. Write a comparison of the two in which you consider the similarities and differences between them. You should write about what the poets say and the structure, language and literary techniques (like rhythm, rhyme, metaphor and simile) that they use. Which of the poems do you find more effective in communicating its message? Give reasons for your answer.

Plan your response below and write your answer fully on a separate piece of paper.

| Notes and quotations |
| --- |
| |

# Key skills

## Dashes

Hyphens are used to glue words together. Dashes are used to **interrupt**. They can be used instead of brackets to keep topics separate inside the same sentence, or, at the end of direct speech, to indicate somebody stopping speaking abruptly:

— Bigfoot lives in the forests of North America – or so they say.

— I need to buy eggs – I want to make an omelette – but the shop is out of stock.

— 'I can't seem to – oh, look at that – pay attention.'

— 'Don't you dare interrupt me when I'm trying to –' he blustered.

This poem is by the American poet Emily Dickinson (1830–86).

Read through the poem carefully and then answer the questions that follow.

---

## I'm Nobody

I'm Nobody! Who are you?
Are you – Nobody – too?
Then there's a pair of us!
Don't tell! they'd advertise – you know!

5  How dreary – to be – Somebody!
How public – like a Frog –
To tell one's name – the livelong June –
To an admiring Bog!

Emily Dickinson

---

**1**  Explain as fully as you can the impression you gain of the speaker's voice from reading this poem.

..................................................................................................................................................

..................................................................................................................................................

..................................................................................................................................................

..................................................................................................................................................

..................................................................................................................................................

..................................................................................................................................................

..................................................................................................................................................

**2** Write the poem out in sentences with different capitalisation and punctuation – for example commas, semicolons and brackets.

......................................................................................................................................

......................................................................................................................................

......................................................................................................................................

......................................................................................................................................

......................................................................................................................................

......................................................................................................................................

......................................................................................................................................

**3** Now compare your new passage with Dickinson's. Think about:
  – what the dashes did that you have changed
  – how she has used capital letters in the poem
  – any other effects you notice.

Now, on a separate piece of paper, explain how Dickinson has used punctuation in this poem to create effects.

## Synonyms

The two words in each question below have a similar meaning but are not always interchangeable. On a separate piece of paper, write sentences using each of the words in order to illustrate their different shades of meaning.

**1** angry / furious

**2** devour / graze

**3** hardworking / thorough

**4** delighted / pleased

**5** lonely / solitary

**6** run / rush

**7** believe / suspect

**8** exhausted / overworked

## Rhyme and rhythm

Read these two poems about nature.

### Who Has Seen the Wind?

Who has seen the wind?
Neither I nor you.
But when the leaves hang trembling,
The wind is passing through.

5   Who has seen the wind?
Neither you nor I.
But when the trees bow down their heads,
The wind is passing by.

Christina Rossetti

### Afternoon on a Hill

I will be the gladdest thing
Under the sun!
I will touch a hundred flowers
And not pick one.

5   I will look at cliffs and clouds
With quiet eyes,
Watch the wind bow down the grass,
And the grass rise.

And when lights begin to show
10  Up from the town,
I will mark which must be mine,
And then start down!

Edna St. Vincent Millay

1   Identify the rhyming pattern for each poem by writing a letter at the end of each line.

2   Read the poems aloud and think about where you stress the syllables. Do the poems have a regular metre?

........................................................................................................................

3   Read the poems aloud again. Which rhythm do you prefer? Why?

........................................................................................................................

........................................................................................................................

4   Identify as many features of figurative language from each poem as you can (think about rhetorical questions, alliteration, assonance, sibilance, personification, onomatopoeia). How does the figurative language help with the rhythm of the poem? Write your answer on a separate piece of paper.

5   Finally, read the poems aloud again one last time. Which poem do you prefer and why?

........................................................................................................................

........................................................................................................................

# Writing

## A poem about the environment

Read the poem 'Important Notice' by Philip Waddell on page 72 again. Write your own dramatic poem about the environment – you could focus on extinction of animals, like Waddell, or you could focus on other environmental issues such as plastic in the oceans, climate change or fast fashion.

Plan your poem here first. Think about how you want people to feel when they read your poem – do you want to call your readers to action? Think about the mood, atmosphere and tone you would like to use.

Think about the syllables and words you would like to stress in each line, whether you would like your poem to rhyme or whether it should have a regular or irregular metre. If you are unsure where to start, you could write down key words of your chosen topic and try to find some words, rhymes or phrases to build your poem around. Remember, it always helps to read your poem aloud!

# Reading and listening

## Analysing a speech

This transcript is taken from the end of Barack Obama's victory speech in Chicago on the night he won the US election in 2008.

Read the transcript closely and answer the questions that follow.

This election had many firsts and many stories that will be told for generations. But one that's on my mind tonight is about a woman who cast her ballot in Atlanta. She's a lot like the millions of others who stood in line to make their voice heard in this election except for one thing: Ann Nixon Cooper is 106 years old.

5   She was born just a generation past slavery; a time when there were no cars on the road or planes in the sky; when someone like her couldn't vote for two reasons – because she was a woman and because of the colour of her skin.

And tonight, I think about all that she's seen throughout her century in America – the heartache and the hope; the struggle and the progress; the times we were told that we can't, and the people who
10  pressed on with that American creed: yes we can.

At a time when women's voices were silenced and their hopes dismissed, she lived to see them stand up and speak out and reach out for the ballot. Yes we can.

When there was despair in the dust bowl and depression across the land, she saw a nation conquer fear itself with a New Deal, new jobs, a new sense of common purpose. Yes we can.

15  When the bombs fell on our harbour and tyranny threatened the world, she was there to witness a generation rise to greatness; and a democracy was saved. Yes we can.

She was there for the buses in Montgomery, the hoses in Birmingham, a bridge in Selma, and a preacher from Atlanta who told the people that we shall overcome. Yes we can.

A man touched down on the moon. A wall came down in Berlin. A world was connected by our own
20  science and imagination. And this year, in this election, she touched her finger to a screen, and cast her vote, because after 106 years in America, through the best of times and the darkest of hours, she knows how America can change. Yes we can.

America, we have come so far. We have seen so much. But there is so much more to do. So tonight, let us ask ourselves: if our children should live to see the next century; if my daughters should be so lucky
25  to live as long as Ann Nixon Cooper; what change will they see? What progress will we have made?

This is our chance to answer that call. This is our moment. This is our time to put our people back to work and open doors of opportunity for our kids; to restore prosperity and promote the cause of peace; to reclaim the American dream and reaffirm that fundamental truth, that out of many, we are one; that while we breathe, we hope. And where we are met with cynicism and doubts and those who
30  tell us that we can't, we will respond with that timeless creed that sums up the spirit of a people:

Yes we can.

Barack Obama

You can find this speech on the internet by searching for 'Obama yes we can Chicago'. This part of the speech starts from about 13 minutes. You can watch it and listen to it to help you answer the following questions:

1 What is the purpose of the speech? What evidence do you have for your decision?

...........................................................................................................................................

...........................................................................................................................................

2 Who is the audience, and how can you tell?

...........................................................................................................................................

...........................................................................................................................................

3 What is the main theme of the speech?

...........................................................................................................................................

...........................................................................................................................................

4 Now annotate the transcript with your notes on Obama's language and speaking technique:

   a Where does he place his emphasis, and what techniques does he use to do this? Think about how he uses pauses, volume, rhythm and body language.

   b What linguistic techniques does he use to make his point clearly and keep his audience interested? Look out for devices like repetition, the way the speech is organised, and lists of three.

   c Are there any carefully chosen words which stand out to you, and what reasons can you think of for his choices? Why does he say, 'Yes we can' rather than 'You can do this', or 'This is possible', for example?

5 Now write and deliver your own speech evaluating Obama's historic speech. Think about the following questions: If you were in the audience for this speech, do you think Obama's message would stick with you? Would you remember the main theme of his speech the next day, and would you agree with it? Why, or why not? What did you think was good and bad about Obama's speech, and what do you think he could have done better? Use evidence from your notes, the transcript and the video to help you give your opinion.

Once you have written your speech, deliver it to a friend, family member or neighbour and record yourself doing so. Ask for feedback and ask them to sum up your main opinions on Obama's speech to check you delivered your ideas and opinions clearly.

# Key skills

## How is a play performed?

*Romeo and Juliet* is one of Shakespeare's best-known tragedies. It is a five-act play about a young man named Romeo, from a family called the Montagues, and Juliet, from a family called the Capulets. The two families are locked in a bitter feud.

This is an abridged extract from Act 2. Romeo is hiding in Juliet's garden. He has just been to a party at the Capulets' house in disguise, where he met Juliet for the first time.

Read the script closely to make sure you know what is happening – reading the scene aloud might help – then work on the activity that follows.

## Extract: *Romeo and Juliet*

[*Juliet appears above at a window.*]

**ROMEO:** But soft, what light through yonder window breaks?

It is the east and Juliet is the sun!

Arise, fair sun, and kill the envious moon,

Who is already sick and pale with grief

That thou her maid art\* far more fair than she.

It is my lady, O, it is my love!

O that she knew she were!

She speaks, yet she says nothing; what of that?

Her eye discourses\*, I will answer it.

I am too bold: 'tis not to me she speaks.

See how she leans her cheek upon her hand

O that I were a glove upon that hand,

That I might touch that cheek!

**Juliet:** Ay me!

**Romeo:** She speaks.

O, speak again, bright angel, for thou art

As glorious to this night, being o'er my head,

As is a winged messenger of heaven.

**Juliet:** O Romeo, Romeo! wherefore\* art thou Romeo?

Deny thy father and refuse thy name;

Or, if thou will not, be but sworn my love,

And I'll no longer be a Capulet.

| Romeo: | [*Aside.*] Shall I hear more, or shall I speak at this? |
|---|---|
| Juliet: | 'Tis but thy* name that is my enemy: |
| | Thou art thyself, though not a Montague. |
| | What's Montague? It is nor hand, nor foot, |
| | Nor arm, nor face, nor any other part |
| | Belonging to a man. O, be some other name. |
| | What's in a name? That which we call a rose |
| | By any other name would smell as sweet; |
| | So Romeo would, were he not Romeo called, |
| | Retain that dear perfection which he owes |
| | Without that title. Romeo, doff* thy name, |
| | And for that name, which is no part of thee, |
| | Take all myself. |
| Romeo: | I take thee at thy word. |
| | Call me but love, and I'll be new baptised; |
| | Henceforth I never will be Romeo. |
| Juliet: | How came thou hither, tell me, and wherefore? |
| | The orchard walls are high and hard to climb, |
| | And the place death, considering who thou art, |
| | If any of my kinsmen find thee here. |
| Romeo: | With love's light wings did I o'erperch these walls, |
| | For stony limits cannot hold love out, |
| | And what love can do, that dares love attempt: |
| | Therefore thy kinsmen are no stop to me. |
| Juliet: | If they do see thee, they will murder thee. |
| Romeo: | My life were better ended by their hate |
| | Than death prorogued*, wanting of thy love. |

* *thou art: you are*

*discourses: speaks*

*wherefore: why*

*thy: your*

*doff: take off*

*prorogued: postponed*

1 When do Romeo and Juliet start talking to each other, rather than to themselves? Mark that point on the script.

2 What is the main idea in this part of the script? In your own words, summarise what the characters are talking about.

.......................................................................................................................................................

.......................................................................................................................................................

3 How do you think this scene will contribute to the overall plot? What dramatic irony or foreshadowing can you find to help you predict what might happen?

.......................................................................................................................................................

.......................................................................................................................................................

4 What do the characters' words tell you about them? What kind of personalities do they have? Find a key line that tells you something about each character and note down next to it what it reveals.

5 Imagine you are the director of this scene and think carefully about how you would like it to be acted and performed in front of your classmates.

   a Shakespearian language can be hard for modern audiences to follow. How would you make clear what the characters are saying and feeling in this scene, to help your audience? Are there any words or phrases you would want to be emphasised? Would you give the actors any particular actions or movements? Would you want them to shout or whisper any lines? Annotate your script with stage directions for your actors.

   b On a separate piece of paper, make notes on what sets, props, lighting, sound effects and costumes you would choose. Look for clues in the script to justify your choices – how might Juliet be dressed, based on how Romeo describes her? Where have the characters just been? What time of day is it?

6 Find a video of another adaptation of this scene online (search for 'Romeo and Juliet balcony scene'). What do you think of the director's and actors' choices? Think about what audience the adaptation was made for. Write down whether you agree with the choices the director has made. Use evidence from the script in your answer.

.......................................................................................................................................................

.......................................................................................................................................................

.......................................................................................................................................................

.......................................................................................................................................................

**7** Write down three pieces of advice you would give to the actor playing Romeo in the adaptation you watched that would help you understand his performance more.

.......................................................................................................................

.......................................................................................................................

.......................................................................................................................

# Writing and speaking

## A speech about an endangered animal

Look back at the article that you wrote about an endangered animal on page 43. Think about how you could make the same points in a short speech, using some of the techniques you have analysed. How would you make sure your audience would remember your most important points? When would you keep your sentences short, and when would you make them longer?

Plan your speech below and then, on a separate piece of paper, write a full transcript of your speech, considering your punctuation and paragraphs carefully to help you remember where to pause. Make sure you write clearly so that you can read your handwriting when you speak!

Make notes on where you would speed up, slow down and get louder or quieter to make your point memorably. Would you use any other body language? How might you move, gesture or use non-verbal communication?

Practise reading your speech out loud in front of a mirror, or record and watch yourself, to check that your instructions to yourself work. Then deliver it to an audience!

To practise delivering your speech to different audiences, you could firstly deliver it to somebody in your age group, or a small group from your class, who you think will be sympathetic to your points. Then, find somebody who you think does not know much about endangered animals or might not be sympathetic to your concerns. How will you adapt your communication for each audience?

Don't forget that your audience will not be able to read your notes so they will be relying on watching and listening to you.

.......................................................................................................................

.......................................................................................................................

.......................................................................................................................

.......................................................................................................................

.......................................................................................................................

.......................................................................................................................

# Revision

To involve and engage readers, writers use a range of structural, linguistic and literary features. You can find more about these features by referring to the Stage 7 Student Book but to remind you here are the main features:

**Structural features**: in particular, when discussing the structure of a piece of writing, you should consider the writer's focus or viewpoint, the opening and closing of the piece of writing, the use of contrast and repetition, the way events are ordered, the use of dialogue, variations in the length of sentences and paragraphs, the use of headings, and sub-headings in a non-fiction piece.

**Linguistic features**: the tone and register used by the writer, the use of formal and informal expression, the tense in which the passage is written and the vocabulary used – for example, simple or complex.

**Literary features**: the writer's use of a range of figurative language such as similes, metaphors, onomatopoeia, hyperbole, assonance, alliteration, sibilance, anaphora, etc.

Here are three pieces of writing: the first is a poem, the second a non-fiction passage and the third an extract from a novel. Read all of them carefully and then answer the questions that follow.

---

## Hurricane Hits England

*Grace Nichols is a Guyanese poet who has lived in the south of England since 1977. This area of the country was hit by an unexpected hurricane in 1987, which caused widespread, substantial damage. In this poem Grace Nichols gives her response to this event and how it brings back memories of the Caribbean area where she was born and lived as a child.*

It took a hurricane, to bring her closer
To the landscape.
Half the night she lay awake,
The howling ship of the wind,
5   Its gathering rage,
Like some dark ancestral spectre.
Fearful and reassuring.

Talk to me Huracan
Talk to me Oya
10  Talk to me Shango*
And Hattie,
My sweeping, back-home cousin.

Tell me why you visit
An English coast?
15  What is the meaning
Of old tongues
Reaping havoc
In new places?

Oya is an African Goddess with the power to create storms; Shango is her husband and God of thunder and lightning.

Hurricane Hattie was one of the strongest and deadliest tropical cyclones of the 1961 Atlantic hurricane season.

The blinding illumination,
20 Even as you short-
Circuit us
Into further darkness?

What is the meaning of trees
Falling heavy as whales
25 Their crusted roots
Their cratered graves?

O why is my heart unchained?
Tropical Oya of the Weather,
I am aligning myself to you,
30 I am following the movement of your winds,
I am riding the mystery of your storm.

Ah, sweet mystery,
Come to break the frozen lake in me,
Shaking the foundations of the very trees within me,
35 Come to let me know
That the earth is the earth is the earth.

Grace Nichols

# What Should You See In Kyoto?

Kyoto is a slice of traditional Japan and a snapshot to the past. Though the lively bars and restaurants show the modern side of Kyoto, its shrines and temples are the heart and soul of its ancient past. Kyoto is a must-see city, with over 17 UNESCO World Heritage sites, 1600 Buddhist temples and countless Shinto shrines.

5 From bamboo forests to traditional tea ceremonies and beguiling geisha, Kyoto is the cultural gem in Japan's crown. There are so many things to do and we've only picked out a handful of our highlights here. Our advice is to take your time to explore, visit as much as you can and enjoy the journey!

## Some things to see in Kyoto

### Arashiyama Bamboo Grove

Arashiyama is a magical district brimming with mountain trails, temples, gardens and parks. It is
10 home to Tenryu-ji temple, one of the 14 World Heritage Sites in Kyoto. But one of the biggest reasons sightseers flock to Arashiyama is to see the bamboo grove. The trees stretch on into the sky and hypnotise everybody who stops to look. We suggest that you take your photos straight away so you can just stop and soak in the magical atmosphere. You will be amazed!

### Okochi Sanso Garden

15 While you're in Arashiyama and have had your fill of the bamboo grove, we recommend visiting this hidden gem of a garden. You have to pay an entrance fee but you get a free matcha tea and traditional Japanese sweet at the end of the walk, which makes it well worth it! The garden used to belong to film director Okochi Denjiro. It is such a blissful lull away from the winding groves of Arashiyama.

20 ### Fushimi Inari-taisha Shrine

Fushimi Inari Shrine is the ultimate torii gate experience and is the most important of several thousand shrines dedicated to Inari, the Shinto god of rice. While most people come to explore the mountain trails, the shrines themselves are amazing to see too. We arrived late in the afternoon and had to almost sprint up the hill as the evening darkness closed in on us, but the lights come on and
25 cast a shadow through the gates. It was breath-taking. It is a long walk (it took us 2–3 hours!) so make sure you have good walking shoes, but it's well worth the effort.

### Gion Kyoto

Gion is the most famous district in Kyoto and is where most people picture when they think of the capital. With many of its streets unchanged in over 300 years, it is here you can catch a glimpse of
30 geisha walking around in traditional costume and ancient tea houses serving you delicious teas. Gion really lights up at night with its glowing lanterns and bustling restaurants and bars, so we definitely recommend a visit when the sun goes down.

### Where should I stay?

There are many great hotels and apartments in Kyoto. Read the post below to find out more.
35 Where to stay

Do you have experiences of Kyoto to share? Send us your thoughts using the comments box below.

# Extract: *The Island of Dr Moreau*

*In this passage (written in 1896) the narrator is trying to escape from a terrifying creature created by the mad scientist, Dr Moreau.*

A twig snapped behind me, and there was a rustle. I turned, and stood facing the dark trees. I could see nothing – or else I could see too much. Every dark form in the dimness had its ominous quality, its peculiar suggestion of alert watchfulness. So I stood for perhaps a minute, and then, with an eye to the trees still, turned westward to cross the headland; and as I moved, one among the lurking shadows
5 moved to follow me.

My heart beat quickly. Presently the broad sweep of a bay to the westward became visible, and I halted again. The noiseless shadow halted a dozen yards from me. A little point of light shone on the further bend of the curve, and the grey sweep of the sandy beach lay faint under the starlight. Perhaps two miles away was that little point of light. To get to the beach I should have to go through
10 the trees where the shadows lurked, and down a bushy slope.

I could see the Thing rather more distinctly now. It was no animal, for it stood erect. At that I opened my mouth to speak, and found a hoarse phlegm choked my voice. I tried again, and shouted, "Who is there?" There was no answer. I advanced a step. The Thing did not move, only gathered itself together. My foot struck a stone. That gave me an idea. Without taking my eyes off the black form
15 before me, I stooped and picked up this lump of rock; but at my motion the Thing turned abruptly as a dog might have done, and slunk obliquely into the further darkness. Then I recalled a schoolboy expedient against big dogs, and twisted the rock into my handkerchief, and gave this a turn round my wrist. I heard a movement further off among the shadows, as if the Thing was in retreat. Then suddenly my tense excitement gave way; I broke into a profuse perspiration and fell a-trembling, with
20 my adversary routed and this weapon in my hand.

It was some time before I could summon resolution to go down through the trees and bushes upon the flank of the headland to the beach. At last I did it at a run; and as I emerged from the thicket upon the sand, I heard some other body come crashing after me. At that I completely lost my head with fear, and began running along the sand. Forthwith there came the swift patter of soft feet in
25 pursuit. I gave a wild cry, and redoubled my pace. Some dim, black things about three or four times the size of rabbits went running or hopping up from the beach towards the bushes as I passed.

So long as I live, I shall remember the terror of that chase. I ran near the water's edge, and heard every now and then the splash of the feet that gained upon me. Far away, hopelessly far, was the yellow light. All the night about us was black and still. Splash, splash, came the pursuing feet, nearer
30 and nearer. I felt my breath going, for I was quite out of training; it whooped as I drew it, and I felt a pain like a knife at my side. I perceived the Thing would come up with me long before I reached the enclosure, and, desperate and sobbing for my breath, I wheeled round upon it and struck at it as it came up to me,— struck with all my strength.

H. G. Wells

1  Identify the main structural, linguistic and literary features used in each of the three pieces of writing and discuss how they affect the reader. Use the space below to plan your answer then write your response on a separate piece of paper.

.......................................................................................................................................

.......................................................................................................................................

.......................................................................................................................................

.......................................................................................................................................

.......................................................................................................................................

.......................................................................................................................................

.......................................................................................................................................

.......................................................................................................................................

2  How do the structural, linguistic and literary features you identified in question 1 differ? With reference to the purpose, context and audience for each text, discuss how this affects the use of features. Use the space below to plan your answer then write your response on a separate piece of paper.

.......................................................................................................................................

.......................................................................................................................................

.......................................................................................................................................

.......................................................................................................................................

.......................................................................................................................................

.......................................................................................................................................

.......................................................................................................................................

.......................................................................................................................................

# Cambridge checkpoint

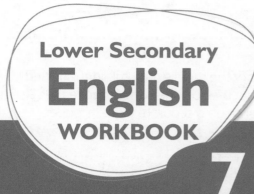

## Lower Secondary English WORKBOOK 7

Reinforce learning and challenge students to develop their learning further with this Workbook.

● **Provide extra practice:** Each Workbook is intended to be used by students for homework and further practice, enabling their skillset to develop and grow. Once completed the Workbook can be kept and used for revision.

● **Develop understanding and build confidence:** Write-in activities help gauge the level of understanding and test a range of skills in reading, writing and speaking and listening.

● **Engage students and extend understanding:** A range of topical and stimulating activities to help extend reading and listening skills, which encourage students to engage with political, historical and cultural contexts in the world around them.

For over 25 years we have been trusted by Cambridge schools around the world to provide quality support for teaching and learning. For this reason we have been selected by Cambridge Assessment International Education as an official publisher of endorsed material for their syllabuses.

Working for over **25 YEARS** WITH Cambridge Assessment International Education

This resource is endorsed by Cambridge Assessment International Education

✓ Provides learner support as part of a set of resources for the Cambridge Lower Secondary English curriculum framework (0861) from 2020

✓ Has passed Cambridge International's rigorous quality-assurance process

✓ Developed by subject experts

✓ For Cambridge schools worldwide

## Boost
This series includes eBooks and teacher support.
Visit www.hoddereducation.com/boost to find out more.

Registered Cambridge International Schools benefit from high-quality programmes, assessments and a wide range of support so that teachers can effectively deliver Cambridge Lower Secondary.

Visit **www.cambridgeinternational.org/ lowersecondary** to find out more.

## HODDER EDUCATION
e: education@hachette.co.uk
w: hoddereducation.com

ISBN 978-1-398-30133-7

9 781398 301337

FSC www.fsc.org
MIX
Paper from responsible sources
FSC™ C104740